Bodhi

Jeffrey M Dullum

INTRODUCTION

"Are you going to snort this?" I asked, as I looked away from the shaman and turned to Nate.

"You don't snort it. You exhale, then he blows it into your nostril," Nate answered calmly with a smile. "And no, I don't do this part anymore."

"That good? Then I am doing this," I said, as I returned the smile, then turned back to the shaman with my game face on.

The shaman who stood in front of me, in his early 40's, had black, shoulder length hair and a thick beard with shades of grey.

He wore an off-white, long-sleeved shirt that sported a bright, silver and gold embroidered print around the neck and shoulders areas, then faded down onto the open chest and baggy sleeves. This shirt resembled a tablecloth with the shaman's head as a centerpiece.

I instantly had great respect for this man, since he was about to blow my mind with the bottle rocket shaped bamboo stick that he held in his left hand.

As if he was beginning to conduct an orchestra, he tilted his head back, raised his chin, and lowered his opened right hand down the center of his chest towards his belly. Then he raised the bamboo stick in his left hand towards my right nostril, and said something in Spanish.

"What?...should I breathe? What did he say?" I asked, as I turned to Nate, totally throwing the whole ceremony out of rhythm.

"He told you to exhale. He'll breathe for you when he blows through the bamboo," Nate said quietly.

I turned back to the master, closed my eyes, exhaled, and "BAM!"

It felt like he blew a small dart into my forehead.

I could taste it in my throat. It was a little harsh, perhaps some kind of a ritualistic herb for cleansing.

It felt good.

"One more? One more please? Do the other side," I begged, as I pointed to my left nostril.

By now two others, a couple in their early thirties, had entered the large square family room in the shaman's home.

"What's this? I asked, as a small white ceramic bowl was handed to me.

Inside the bowl was a sage green, dry powdered substance and a small ceramic spoon.

"Take a scoop, then tilt your head sideways and pour it into your cheek, pinch it between your cheek and gum, like chewing tobacco. Then suck on it, it should last awhile," Nate instructed.

I picked up the small ceramic spoon, scooped, then poured a teaspoonful into my left cheek.

It tasted grassy.

By now there were ten of us who sat on yoga mats on the hard floor with legs crossed, meditation style, forming a twelve foot diameter circle in the room.

The shaman sat at 12:00. To his left sat the smiling couple in their thirties, and another couple to their left. I was sitting at 5:00, with a pleasant woman to my left who was straight across from the shaman, then Nate, then a younger, thin girl in her twenties, then the shaman's wife, who held a cinnamon brown cat in her arms.

The email invitation had asked each attendee to bring a snack to share after the session.

Everyone in the room spoke Spanish except me. I greeted them each with a handshake. We placed the snacks, which included locally grown bananas, a large mason jar of kombucha tea for all to pass and share, a loaf of organic brown bread to be broken amongst the group and a large wooden salad bowl, stocked with Cheetos in the center of the circle.

Just as I was thinking *"Am I high, or is that a giant bowl of fucking Cheetos?"* the lady sitting to my left handed me a small, four ounce glass jar, that had a chocolate brown pasty substance inside of it. She motioned for me to place my index finger inside the jar and scoop out a fingerful, then place the paste on my tongue.

"What is it?" I whispered.

Nate who overheard, leaned forward, turned to me and said quietly "It's organic, made from the coca leaf."

When I heard the word "organic," I tried to stuff two fingers into the jar. But both fingers didn't fit thru the opening, so instead, like a rat in a cage, I scooped really fast with one finger, wiped it onto my tongue, smiled at the woman, then double-dipped and scooped again.

We were about to get started.

Like using a final basketball timeout, just before the shaman began, I leaned forward in my sitting position, reached out and grabbed the small bowl of light green powder, and poured another scoop into my cheek.

Now I was ready.

The shaman's wife had dimmed the lights. The shaman held out in the palm of his hand, a small, six inch diameter, copper Tibetan sound bowl with small black triangles painted on it.

He began to chant slowly.

In the same rhythm that he chanted, he held a wand-like object in his right hand and stroked it slowly around the outside of the bowl.

The sound was so pure that it didn't seem real.

As the shaman played his bowl instrument, and chanted and sang in Spanish, I peeked through my eyelids noticing everyone else had their eyes closed too, except the master.

As the shaman continued, my eyes became heavy and began to close, but not before I noticed everyone else was now stretched out flat on their backs on the yoga mats.

I did the same, and closed my eyes.

The shaman's voice hummed and chanted Spanish words.

I did not understand the Spanish words literally, however, energetically, every sound and word resonated throughout my body. As I lay there, I felt my body vibrating to those sounds and tones.

My eyelids were closed, but they felt so light and translucent, that I could see shadows and figures dancing on the ceiling in the room.

I sensed the shaman as he stood and started walking slowly around inside our circle.

I could hear his voice become louder as he walked past me, then fade as he continued walking around and around.

He was, with us, creating a spiritual vortex of resistant free energy.

Within minutes I could no longer feel my feet.

I heard the sound of crackling fire and smelled smoke as he walked around and around holding an object that I sensed was shaped like a torch.

I could smell and hear that he was burning a torch of incense made from a plant or herb. It had a pleasant odor that smelled like sandalwood.

I could see his shadow holding the torch as he passed by me but I could not lift my eyelids to look.

My mind had now completely left my body.

I was pure consciousness.

Around and around the energy flowed.

The sounds and vibrations became more and more and began taking shape as his beautiful voice became louder and louder.

The vibrations formed a funnel-shaped image that began to rotate and spin. Faster and faster it spun as it fed off its own momentum.

It was a silver and white tornado, a vortex, that was twisting, swirling and spinning right above my head.

It was pure positive, resistance free energy strumming my body like a musical instrument and opening my mind to a virtual reality dream world that was now expanding in my mind with images of my brother and dad laughing, smiling, pointing at me, in non-physical form.

I was matching the frequency of the non-physical and the dream world.

It felt incredible, like I was alive, awake, living inside my own dream.

More scenes began appearing, projected onto the inner walls of the vortex as it spun.

And, as if I was watching a film, I could see and hear the voices and sounds from the vortex walls, but I could not interact.

The tornado was vibrating, humming, orbiting and harmonizing at a very high frequency.

It was a love tornado.

I would have to match that frequency and release all resistance for it to take me in.

Suddenly, I was inside…

A Texan, a preacher, a Mexican and an Irishman walk into a bar, in the desert.

The Texan says "Aloha brah! Welcome to the ship, Jeffrey! Y'all have a shot on me!"

Then the preacher says "What you should do Jeff, is take that red Lamborghini, put it in gear, then light it on fire and send it over a cliff!"

"Mista Jayff, where's my shot?" says the Mexican.

I'm bartending, in a desert, on a ship called "Alicia."

The tall Irishman throws back his head of long black hair, bursts into laughter, and says "You've never heard of Paddy McGinty's Goat?! Ha! Ha! Ha!" he roars. "Give me a Redd!"

The vortex walls keep spinning, swirling and changing scenes.

Next, I'm on stage playing guitar and singing live with a giant drummer who's wearing a small green hat in a little record shack. The drummer, as tall as the ceiling sporting a long black beard, sleeveless t-shirt and barbed wire tattoo, stands up from his tiny stool and commands in his booming baritone voice "Find the girl who has eyes like this!" as he points to the other side of the spinning vortex.

I turn, look, and there I am. I'm sitting at a bar, drinking a beer. A bartender appears...

"Sure, I'll be in your movie, I just don't know if I will be very good at it," says a young Latina bartender who possesses the unspeakable beauty of a Disney princess. "But I'll drive the Lamborghini!" she continues smiling. Then she fades like vapor thru the vortex wall as it spins.

It's spinning faster and faster as another scene appears.

"Lose the girl, you must lose the girl, it's a love tornado! You must lose her! It is the best part!" says an Italian wedding photographer, who is directing and taking pictures of me leaving, not marrying, an incredibly gorgeous Latina supermodel.

Our clasped hands separate at the corner of a majestic castle wall near the ocean.

And then, she's gone.

The love tornado's momentum is now at its most powerful.

A dancer appears.

She takes my hands and counts "one, two, three...five, six, seven," as we dance.

Her hips flow smoothly, effortlessly to the rhythm of the vortex. Her richly accented voice, exotic beauty, grace and sexiness are deeply intoxicating.

As we dance, I cross step to the side as we hold hands. As she passes in front of me for a spin, my right hand releases her left hand.

Simultaneously, I raise my left hand, and holding her right hand above her head, I spin her.

As her right hand rotates inside the palm of my left hand while she is spinning, a ring slides off her right finger, and begins to fall.

The ring falls in slow motion through the air towards the bottom of the vortex.

I look down at the ring, then back at her. She says "The ring is too big. The ring does not fit, I am not the one," she continues.

I try to tell her she is...

She turns her head in sadness...

It's a dream, I have no voice, no words...I can't tell her...I start to panic...I can't breathe...communication lost...she can't hear me...I'm losing her...

...the energy shifts.

...the vortex fades.

...I try to TELL HER.

The vortex is gone.

"Whoa….that...seemed so real," I thought, as I awoke from a deep sleep and popped up in the back of my Ford Focus wagon.

Where the hell am I? I thought.

I climbed out of the back of my car and slipped on my shoes.

It was dawn. I stood on the shoulder of the two-lane desert highway, took a piss and tried to remember where I was.

I got back in my car and started driving.

The first road sign I approached said:

"Welcome to Texas!"

CHAPTER 1

I continued heading southeast on the barren two-lane highway.

The sun rose.

I passed oil rigs, cotton fields and a town called Happy, and soon arrived in a city called Lubbock.

"I'm here." I sent a text to Damin.

As I drove into town, I saw signs and logos that boasted "Home of Texas Tech University."

Then I saw a Starbucks Coffee store.

Nice. There was something about the Starbucks sign that gave me comfort, a feeling of home in this strange land.

The exterior of the Starbucks looked as if it had just withstood a hit from a small twister. The siding, sidewalks and railings were caked with a light brown, sandy dust.

As I walked through the parking lot I noticed the place was just trashed. Solo cups, aluminum cans, straws, plastic lids and bags that had been blasted by the wind, now lay scattered across the paved roads and concrete sidewalks.

It was a late Sunday morning and either everyone was in church or there had been a recent apocalypse, because there was no one in or around the coffee shop.

What am I doing here? I thought, as I entered the store.

As I received my Venti Pike from the barista, the only person around, she brought me up to speed. I was on the college campus of Texas Tech, which had just recessed for spring break over the weekend.

The place had been partying.

"Where are you?" I looked at my phone and read the text.

"Starbucks, on campus." I texted back.

"I'll be right there." Damin responded.

As I stood outside in the parking lot sipping my hot brew in the warm sun, I quickly turned my head to the sound of squealing tires, dual exhaust and a screaming muscle car.

A smiling, energetic face appeared behind the wheel of this smoking hot, red, 71 Chevelle SS as it squawked into a parking space.

The tall, lean, handsome, shaggy black-haired driver wearing a TT ball cap and Ray-Bans jumped out of this vehicle, that with its bold white stripes, looked identical to the one on Starsky and Hutch.

"Aloha brah? How y'all doing?" said the Texas Haole with an Italian name.

"Pellizarri!" I said, as he got out of the car. We exchanged a handshake and bro-hug.

"Like my ride?" he asked, and laughed heartily.

"Leave your car here and get in. We're gonna meet Alicia for lunch and then stop by Mushroom Matt's on our way out of town. But first, we're going to the head shop, I need a pipe!" he said.

"Gardski's?" I asked.

"Oh ya, this is their last day. Tomorrow they're moving everything out so we can start gutting the place, let's go," he said.

We drove to Broadway Street, pulled into a parking lot, then walked through the front door of an old building that said "Gardski's" above the entrance.

The structure looked very much like a large house that had been turned into a restaurant.

The front of the house faced Broadway Street and had an enormous, steep gable end for a roof line.

A smaller dormer size gable, supported by wooden pillars and beams, extended outward below the large gable. This lower gable, reached out and covered an outdoor patio.

"This way, follow me," Damin said, as we passed the dining room that was thinly carpeted in forest green, maroon, beige and black, like a movie theatre from the '70's. This room was hosting guests, sitting at tables eating Sunday brunch.

"Shhhh...upstairs," he said.

As I followed him up a wooden spiral staircase with white hand railings and balusters, he turned and whispered "These guests have no idea that this place is gone tomorrow."

At the top of the stairs we turned left and through a narrow doorway into a small boutique, cigar style bar called Gardski's Loft. The room was dark, furnished with worn leather couches and card tables. Old black and white photos framed in antique brass hung throughout the room.

Three cathedral stained glass windows lightly dappled the room with crisp, colorful, filtered sunlight.

"Two Shiner Bochs," Damin said to a stoic looking male bartender dressed in black, as we sat down at the only two stools at the bar.

"This beer is brewed in Shiner, Texas. Cheers, brah," he said.

As our bottles collided, he said "In the '70's this place was hit by a tornado. A server was pinned to the floor when a damaged beam fell on her hair. She was alright. That picture is a photo of it after it was struck." He pointed to a picture of the damaged building that hung on the wall.

"This place is haunted." He laughed, then said "But by the time we're done with it, I'm gonna be the GM and you're gonna be my bartender."

We drove back across town to a sports bar called Cujo's. A pretty blonde woman, Damin's girlfriend, was waiting for us at a table.

"Alicia, this is Jeff! Jeff, this is Alicia!" said Damin.

In a heavy Texas accent, with a pleasant smile she said "Hello Jeff, nice to meet you."

I could see why he liked her. She was sweet as pie.

After a little small talk she said "I've heard a lot of stories about you guys in Maui, I'm sure glad I didn't know y'all at the time!"

"Ma'am, if it wasn't for Maui, we wouldn't be the gentlemen we are today," I said jokingly.

"Ya right," she said rolling her eyes.

We finished lunch, went to get a pipe at Head Hunters Smoke Shop, then drove back to Starbucks to pick up my car.

"Follow me to Matt's," he said.

We entered an apartment on an upper floor of a complex on the southeast side of town.

Matt lived there with his girlfriend Julie and his dog Missy, a corgi.

Matt was an Irish kid with a hair style and beard that made him resemble a young Conor McGregor, Julie was a cute, quiet, adventurous, tattooed, black haired rocker.

After a brief introduction, Matt and Damin started talking about germination, starters and lighting for the psilocybin mushrooms Matt was growing in his apartment. He had a couple crops sprouting in two plastic trays, the size of cookie sheets.

"They were getting tall until Missy ate the whole crop last Thursday...that dog was tripping!" he laughed.

Soon, I was back in my Ford Focus, following Damin in the red Chevelle, and Matt, Julie and Missy in a black Jeep Wrangler with a "No Bad Days" sticker on it. We were heading to a farm in Afton.

I tried to wrap my head around the reality I was now

experiencing as we caravanned across the plains on the two-hour trip to Afton.

Just three weeks earlier I had released my book, The Secret Beast, in paperback, while I was roofing and painting in Washington state.

In The Secret Beast, the dream was created. The dream included a castle, a red Lamborghini, and a beautiful Latina woman.

I'm supposed to be living my dream now and watching it all unfold in my lap. It must happen for my next book Doppelganger. Is this it? Is it happening right now? Am I alive, aware, living inside of my own dream? Well, something needs to happen soon because as of this moment I have no idea where I'm even sleeping tonight.

Damin and I, whom I had met working at the Paradise Grill restaurant in Maui, had become pretty good friends. We both left Maui within weeks of each other in 2013. He went globetrotting with a woman he met in Maui, then back to his hometown in Spur, Texas. I went to Nashville, Tennessee.

I drove back and forth from Nashville to my hometown in Washington state several times. On one occasion, I stopped to visit my daughter while she was living in Big Spring, Texas, about two hours from Lubbock.

Spur, a little north of Big Spring, was also only two hours from Lubbock.

After visiting my daughter, I drove up to Damin's large family ranch in Spur and had beers. At the time, he was doing construction projects with a guy named Ronald.

"I'm thinking about moving into Lubbock to start a business. Thinking about a food truck and running it all over Tech campus and all the events that go on over there," Damin had told me. "I'm also gonna start an aquaponics business, and create a model for people to clone and grow their own organic vegetables without soil. You outta come on down. Hell, one of your daughters is only two hours away."

Damin soon moved to Lubbock, where Alicia was living, and started doing research into the aquaponics culture there.

He met a couple, the Williams, who owned a wholesale/retail grass fed beef business that was doing very well. The Williams wanted to expand and open a restaurant that serves their beef. This was a perfect match with Damin's organic produce ideas.

Damin called to tell me that the Williams were taking over the lease of the historic Gardski's restaurant, that he was going to be the General Contractor of the tenant improvement, and that he was going to be the GM of the restaurant when it was finished. Then he asked me if I wanted to help with the remodel, and then if I wanted to bartend? Well, it got my attention, especially with one of my kids nearby.

The Gardski's project sounded like a whole lot of fun. But I wasn't sure how my dream would manifest, if I chose this path.

After visiting and receiving clarity from Stef, a former co-worker from Paradise Grill in Maui, who was now bartending in Whitefish, Montana, I drove to Lubbock.

"It is not your work to figure out how your dream will manifest, that is the Universe's job!" Stef said.

CHAPTER 2

We arrived at Ronald's place just before sunset.

Ronald was from California and had been in the construction business his whole life. He got tired of the rat race, packed his tools and headed east.

He had several acres on a flat piece of land that had an Afton address, where he lived by himself.

The south end of Ronald's property connected to the north end of Damin's family ranch in Spur. Their properties touched, but they lived in different towns.

But there was no town of Afton, just acres and acres of land.

Ronald lived in a large mobile home that he was remodeling into a more permanent structure. He had a cat, and a young male chocolate lab named Shadow. He had fenced in an area where he raised a few chickens and cows.

He also had tools, acres of tools. Three 40-foot shipping containers were on the property. They held every tool, fastener, fitting, adhesive, compressor, sander, saw, plumbing tool, electrical tool imaginable.

Ronald had a huge metal-roofed shelter that housed his truck, a motorhome, trailers, tractors, blowers, mowers and towers.

"How did he get all this shit here?"

Ronald was a big ol' good looking fella, who stood about 6'4"with a tanned face and dark brown greying hair . He had bad knees from years of doing construction, and was past his prime for laboring all day, but his mind was sharp, really sharp.

After first meeting him, it was easy to see that Ronald had years of knowledge and experience. When it came to construction, he was confident and arrogant, exactly what you need from a lead man. Off the job, the guy would do anything for you.

Damin and Ronald were a good team. Damin knew construction and could sell, sell, sell. Ronald added his wisdom, tools and job experience.

Our plan was to stay the night and load the construction trailer with tools the next day, then drive it to Lubbock and park it in Gardski's parking lot by nightfall. We were to start gutting the interior of the restaurant the following morning, then begin the remodel.

"This place reminds me a little of Hawaii, except without the ocean," I chuckled, as I drank my beer with Damin, Ronald, Matt and Julie while grilling burgers on the barbeque on Ronald's patio.

"Listen! Those are the same doves that were cooing on Maui," I said as we all sat in chairs and stared out at the desert as the sun began to set.

"The temperature, the breeze, the sunset, the birds, all we need is an ocean...and bikinis." I was feeling good.

"I heard that you play music," Ronald said.

"Go get your guitar," Damin echoed.

I had brought my acoustic guitar to Texas and I

needed to practice. I had scheduled a book release show in Gig Harbor for the following month.

I was going to drive back to Washington State and perform an acoustic version of the soundtrack from The Secret Beast and try to sell some books.

After a few beers and a few songs from the soundtrack, a sober Ronald, who doesn't drink, chimed in "Don't you know any covers, or do you just sing your originals?"

And there it was, the social asshole that I came to know and love.

"Let's go to Matador," Damin said. "Chris just texted me, we're all gonna meet up at his bar."

"Nice, what's Matador?" I asked.

"A town just north of here, but we need to stop in Dickens for beer." Damin said.

"Why do we need beer if we're going to a bar?" I said.

"It's his own bar, it's not open to the public," he answered.

"Is his bar in a garage, or in a basement or something?" I asked.

"No, it's right in the middle of downtown. A bunch of our friends are coming, I want you to meet them," he said.

"So we're going to get beer and go party at Chris's bar in downtown Matador, with your friends, at a real bar, that's not open to the public," I confirmed.

"Yep," he said.

It was a real bar, with real bar stools, a real pool table with real dart boards, sofas, neon lights, playing cards, books and games. It stood in the center of a town, population 700, at a main intersection without a traffic light.

The bar had been in Chris's family for three generations. It didn't seem possible to have a bar open to the public in Matador because there were too few people to support one. I didn't see one car drive by all night.

A real bar with real people in it.

We smoked, joked, drank beers, played pool, stood outside and howled to a full moon as thousands of sparkling white stars performed on the biggest, brightest stage I had ever seen in my life. The clear Texas sky.

Was it real or was I dreaming?

I had planned on sleeping in the back of the Focus, but Ronald insisted I sleep in his guest room. Matt and Julie stayed in the motor home, Damin took the couch.

Ronald, with the help of his face-licking chocolate lab Shadow, woke us at 6:00 a.m.

After hours of working in the hot sun, sifting, sorting and rearranging the inventory inside of the shipping containers, we had the construction trailer stocked with the tools we needed to remodel Gardski's.

We returned to Lubbock just before sunset.

We towed the trailer to Gardski's parking lot with Ronald's truck, then headed to Alicia's where she had prepared a steak dinner that was waiting for us.

I had called a few hotels in town to get prices for long term stay. I was prepared to book a room on a weekly basis but hadn't had the chance.

After one of the most satisfying ribeye steaks I had ever eaten, Alicia smiled and said "Jeff, I want to show you something."

"Ya, come on," Damin said, waving to me.

I followed the two of them through the back door of the utility room into a narrow hallway with smooth concrete flooring.

They opened another door at the end of the hallway and entered a large room. As I followed them inside, they turned to me and smiled at the same time. Alicia said "What do you think?"

I was confused and didn't speak.

"This is your new home if you want it!" Damin said.

The garage of her three bedroom, two bath rambler, had been remodeled into a large private bedroom.

It was furnished with a queen size bed that was supported by a sturdy wooden frame. The headboard, which was just as sturdy as the frame, had small shelves built into each end. A brown comforter and white bed-sheets lay folded on the mattress. There was a small square cherry-wood coffee table in one corner of the room. A triangular shaped closet space, without a door, had been built into another corner of the room. A mini fridge was plugged in, ready for beer, just inside the doorway. The room was painted light orange and had a white ceiling fan spinning above the bed.

"It has a private entrance at the end of the hallway. I have a key for you, the code for the alarm is star 1096. It's real quiet out here, so when you want to play your guitar or when y'all have had enough of Damin, you have a place to go," Alicia said with a smile.

I was speechless.

"That's why I wanted you to meet her before we left to Afton, she wanted to make sure you were a decent person," Damin said with a chuckle.

Alicia had a 4 year old son named Dillon who lived there fulltime with her and Damin.

To give a man a bed in his own private room, when he has none, well, there is no greater gift.

In that moment, my whole perspective of my choice to come to Lubbock changed.

"Watch out Matt," I said as I launched the sledge hammer up high and bashed in the top of a wall in the hallway between the kitchen and the bathrooms.

Chunks of hard, painted plaster sprayed from the wall exposing a curtain of chicken wire that supported the plaster on wooden studs.

After exposing this steel, chicken wire mesh, we took shovels, crow bars and claw hammers to rip it from the studs.

Once sheets of the mesh were hanging from the tall,

ten foot walls, we cut it down in pieces with a sawzall.
With one man on each end, we picked up and placed
the heavy slabs on top of a wheelbarrow and wheeled it
down the hallway, through the host station, through the
entrance, down the handicap sidewalk, into the parking
lot on the east side of the building and then up a sloped
ramp into the open end of a twenty foot dumpster.

The plan was to demo the hallway, the GM's office
and the kitchen first. While Matt and I started in the
hallway, Damin, Ronald and Eddy, an electrician who
was brought on fulltime, started deactivating,
unhooking and removing all the kitchen appliances.

Once those rooms were gutted, the dumb waiter that
served the upstairs loft from the kitchen, would be
exposed and ready to be removed.

With every "watch out!" that was yelled in the
hallway from falling walls, there was a "ahhh gross!"
from the kitchen.

Years of grease and neglect spewed out and around
every piece of equipment in the kitchen. We were lucky
to have disposable respirators as dust, insulation and
oldness circulated in the air throughout the entire
building.

Former employees of Gardski's came through the
building throughout our first week of work to pick up
final paychecks. Many of these people were now out of
work and looked at our team and the new owners as the
reason why.

The GM of Gardski's, named George, had been
there twenty-three years. He still came to his office
every day, shut the door and closed himself inside as
we worked. His office was off the hallway between the
kitchen and bathrooms. That room and its walls were

going to be removed to make room to expand the new kitchen.

After five days of demolition, with the sky falling around his office, we finally had to ask him to remove the rest of his belongings and leave.

One of the other managers had been there over ten years. He was a young, tall, good looking Irish lad with long black hair. His name was Sean.

Sean was somewhat in shock over what was happening with his restaurant. He was now out of work, and hung around the building during the first few days. Damin hired him.

Damin also hired a friend from his youth named Ted. Ted was in the navy with Damin. He was in his late thirties, stood six-foot three and was strong as an ox, a brute. He was a welder and was between jobs.

A young homeless man named Jim came in one day. Damin hired him.

Damin ordered lunch every day to be delivered to the restaurant. It was quite a crew that sat on the covered patio and shared stories every day at noon.

One day we ordered pizzas from Giorgio's Pizza. They were too busy to deliver, so I volunteered to pick them up from their shop.

As I was waiting in line to pick up the pizzas, I turned to the wall on my left and saw a framed photo of a red Lamborghini.

I took this sighting as a sign, confirmation. It excited me.

Over the next few days of the demo process, we removed a soda fountain machine from the server's station between the kitchen and main dining area. The drain line from the machine traveled under the server's cabinet and emptied into the main line below the floor. The drain line had a leak and had been dripping soda for years into the crawl space, and had rotted out two of the main weight-bearing floor joists that connected the kitchen and dining room on the ground floor.

Thus far, all of our demolition work had been done without a permit, which we didn't need to begin construction. Permit applications had already been submitted to remove the west, exterior and dining room wall to extend the restaurant into the large parking lot, adding a huge, brand new bar with seating.

The discovery of the damaged floor joists brought all the heads of the project together for a meeting. Mr. Skibell, who owned the building met with the new tenant, the Williams's, Ronald, Damin, Johnny the engineer, and a Lubbock City inspector.

They all stood around the three-foot by eight-foot size hole in the middle of the floor, scratched their heads and came up with a solution. We needed to jack up and support the damaged floor beams, then cut out the damaged wood. A concrete retaining wall then needed to be poured in the crawl space to support new beams to be sistered (installed side by side) into the existing severed beams.

This new work needed to be engineered and permitted before we continued. It would take weeks for the paperwork to be finalized.

As far as timing for my acoustic show in Gig Harbor, this was perfect. I left Lubbock and drove to Washington.

CHAPTER 3

It was mid-morning as I drove northwest on 1-84. I picked up a hitchhiker.

A young man in his late twenties was hitchhiking to a small town called Muleshoe, TX, a few hours from Lubbock.

"What's going on in Muleshoe?" I asked my rider once he was sitting in the front passenger seat.

"I have a friend there I haven't visited in a while. She can't leave the town, so I go see her," he said.

"Why can't she leave? I asked.

"She got busted for smuggling pot. She was set up. She had never done it before and was running a couple pounds for some people and got pulled over. She was used as a decoy so they could run larger quantities through a different route," he said.

"Oh no, so she's in jail, huh?" I asked.

"No. She lives at home and works as a grocery clerk at United Market," he said.

"But she can't leave town? I asked.

"Nope. The judge sentenced her to 10 years in Muleshoe. She can't leave town for 10 years," he said.

"That's harsh," I said.

"I know, that's why I visit her," he said.

Thirty hours later, I arrived in Gig Harbor. I performed my show, sold a few books, then spent the

BODHI

next couple weeks splashing acrylic latex on walls with my brother who's a painting contractor in Seattle.

I kept in contact with Damin almost every day or so for updates on Gardski's.

"Things are moving along just fine with the permits. I got more work for you whenever you decide to head back. The Williams decided to strip and demo the plaster that's covering the ceilings. They have also decided on new lighting and we need to install fire sprinklers. So get your ass down here, we miss ya!" Damin said. "Oh, and you might be interested in this little piece of news. The Williams brought on a chef. He's a bad ass cook from San Antonio. He's gonna be working here bringing in the new kitchen equipment. He's also starting to create the menu. Anyhow, I rented a two bedroom rambler on 35th, it's real close to Gardski's. Brian, the chef, is taking one of the rooms and you are more than welcome to take the other room, or you can stay at Alicia's if you want. We love having you there but thought you might want your own place in the long run, your choice bud!" he said.

I was paying Alicia $75 a week or $300 a month, and my share for the new place with Brian would be $400 a month.

I was so grateful for everything Alicia had done for me. But the next logical step was for me to get my own place.

I immediately left Washington and drove back to Texas.

———————

"Where are you heading? I ask.

33

There was a man in his early 30's sitting next to me in my car as I drive. Another hitchhiker.

"I'm heading back home. I just got off work, I've been out of town for the past couple days doing my route in eastern Washington," he says.

"What kind of route?" I ask.

"I work for a cannabis distributor and we deliver all throughout eastern Washington. It's the best job I've ever had. I drive a brand new Mercedes van stocked with pounds of weed and other cannabis products. I stay at hotels and drive on my own schedule. I've met some great people and usually hang out an extra day and party with them," he boasts.

"That does sound like a great gig," I say.

"I have a couple accounts in Ellensburg near the Central Washington University campus. I went to school there. I laugh because I'm doing the exact same thing I was doing there 10 years ago, selling weed! Except now I'm selling pounds, not grams and I'm driving a brand new Mercedes!" he roars.

I jumped out of my car as I woke from a dream and a quick nap at Love's truck stop just east of Spokane near the Idaho border.

Wow, I dreamt I picked up another hitchhiker. I wonder what that's supposed to mean. I pulled onto 1-90.

Ah, of course, learn from the first one in Muleshoe.

I pulled over just a few miles before the Idaho border and grabbed the gram of bud that I had in my backpack. I stashed it under a freeway overpass at an exit, then continued driving east through Idaho and Montana.

I had forgotten that I had it. My dream reminded me.

Bud is legal in Washington and Colorado but illegal in Idaho and Montana. I preferred not to cross state lines with it. I wasn't prepared to live in Idaho or Montana for 10 years.

I took a picture of the exit for future navigational and locating purposes. If I returned to Washington driving this route, I had a little treat waiting for me, just like I had one waiting for me buried beside a guardrail post on I-25 near the Colorado/New Mexico border.

I returned to Lubbock, moved in with Brian in the rambler Damin had rented and fully furnished for us, and went back to work at Gardski's.

The rental was close to restaurants, parks and within a mile of campus.

I went for a walk the first night in my new neighborhood. It was around 9:00 p.m.

I walked down 35th, crossed Indiana Avenue and through a Walgreens parking lot, and spotted a sports bar called Caprock Café.

From outside, I could see the big screen TVs.

I walked in, feeling like I had entered a dream.

I walked through the outdoor patio and into the air conditioned restaurant. Immediately, I sensed a familiar energy.

I saw an open path through the dining tables that

took me towards the bar. The bar was L-shaped. I walked up to the short side of the L and pulled up a stool.

When the girl who was bartending turned to ask me if I'd like a beer, I smiled and said "Yes."

"Tuesday night is $2.50 for Bud Lights and Wednesday, is Shiners for $3.00," she said, her voice friendly.

It was Tuesday night, and I ordered a Bud Light. It came in a large, icy, frosty glass.

"Y'all new here?" she asked.

"Ya, just moved in a couple blocks from here. I'm Jeff, thanks for the beer," I said.

"Sure, I'm Camila, nice to meet you. Do you want a menu?" she asked with a smile.

"Naw, I'm good, thanks," I said.

She smiled, turned and walked down to the other end of the bar. I was sitting on the end and could see all the seats down the long bar and everything behind the bar.

I had a great view of the big screen in the dining room and a smaller TV at the bar.

After a couple draws from my schooner and a pause to double check my surroundings, I realized that the bartender I'd just spoken too was probably the most beautiful human being I had ever seen. Her long black hair had tints of purple and was parted down middle. She had arched black eyebrows and narrow brown eyes that pierced my heart within seconds. Her rosy red cheek bones sat high above her wide charming smile. Her lips were not full. Her lips were not thin. Her lips were perfect. She wore a white spaghetti strap top that exposed her smooth olive skin and small delicate shoulders. She was wearing high cut black shorts and short black cowboy boots that elevated her 5'3" frame. Her legs made it difficult to sip my beer without spilling.

And the whole scene was just so familiar.

Then it hit me.

She was a clone of Josefina, the bartender I had met in Tacoma at Medi's.

I had just moved to Tacoma and had walked a couple blocks through an alley to 6th Ave. I crossed the street and through the window I saw Josefina bartending.

And now, I had again just moved into a new town and walked a couple blocks to Caprock.

The bar inside Caprock was set-up exactly like Medis, L shaped.

I had walked to the short end of the bar at Medi's and had sat on a barstool when I'd first met Josefina, like I just did at Caprock.

Now I felt the same presence and spirit of my older brother as I did when I met Josefina. He had just died a few months before I had moved to Tacoma and his spirit was very much guiding me. He was laughing then and he was laughing now. It felt like he had set everything up for me, and was having fun watching me discover it. He was having fun teasing me, like older brothers do, just for the entertainment.

I looked up at the wall above the top shelf behind the bar, and I started laughing too.

There hanging high and proud was a giant photo of Coach Mike Leach emerging from the tunnel at Martin Stadium, and running fast with my alma mater and former team, the Washington State Cougars before a football game in Pullman, WA.

My brother had graduated WSU and became an F-15 pilot. He was stationed in Lubbock at Reese Airforce base in the '80's. I had visited him here. I have a niece and nephew that were born in Lubbock.

Ex-Texas Tech coach Leach was now the Coug's new coach. The people in Lubbock absolutely loved Coach Leach, and obviously still do.

I was experiencing deja vu on every level as I tried to process the whole scene.

I was enjoying every sip of my beer.

The bar was now empty.

"What time do you close?" I asked.

"Ten," Camila said.

A clock on the wall said 9:40 and my beer was getting low.

"May I please get one more Bud Light before last call?" I asked.

"Oh, no problem. I still have to close, so I'll probably be here till 11:00. You are more than welcome to stay while I close," she said.

I stayed until 10:45.

CHAPTER 4

It was fall and football season was starting.

Damin brought on Juan, a local multi-talented construction worker and Juan's nephew, Chris. Ted returned to welding, Mushroom Matt moved to New York and Jimmy the homeless man moved on.

We gathered daily at either BarPM, Bashes, Caprock or Gardski's patio for beers after work.

We also built a bar in Alicia's backyard. Damin took a 6'x 9' metal shed, stripped the walls and placed it on a new concrete footing and patio that we poured.

Ronald wired it with power and installed a custom wood bar. A three foot, blue tooth sound bar speaker was mounted on the back wall. It was decorated with a neon sign, strings of colored LED lights that lit up the ceiling, shells, fish nets, a ship wheel, a sailor cap and a giant plastic Parrot painted orange and lime green.

We called it The Ship.

Sean, Juan, Damin, Larry the preacher (Alicia's dad) and myself were regulars. We spent hours partying, listening to music, squeezing every ounce of fun out of our incredible experience together.

"You touched the top of the bottle with your hand when you removed the cap!" Sean said as I handed him his Redd hard cider.

"Always use the bartender key for opening bottles so the customer doesn't have your DNA where their lips go!" said Damin.

I had never bartended before and the Ship was the

beginning of my training. My friends were preparing me for Gardski's.

We were making great progress at the restaurant and the kitchen was finished.

We framed in new walls, replaced tornado damaged ceiling beams that served not only the kitchen but supported the whole upstairs. We wired, plumbed, sheetrocked, painted, installed a suspended ceiling and applied FRP plastic wallboard over sheetrock throughout not only the kitchen, but whole the backend of the building.

We replaced damaged floor joists and installed new tile flooring in the kitchen, hallways and bathrooms. We gutted the plaster, replaced damaged ceiling joists, sheetrocked, painted and finish trimmed the dining room.

We stripped, wired and sheetrocked the upstairs dining room next to the Loft and installed HVAC in the attic.

We refinished the stairway and poured a huge slab of concrete for the new bar and patio.

Gardski's was eighty percent finished, and the Williams had the idea to get everyone who was going to be involved with the restaurant, together for a little fun.

Brian had a food truck, so we fenced in the Gardski's parking lot and threw a tailgate party before a Tech game one Saturday.

I worked behind the bar that we had set up under a tent.

I got my Texas alcohol card and legally poured and sold my first beers ever as a bartender.

A couple days later Camila saw a photo on Facebook with me in it that the restaurant had posted from the tailgate party. She friended me.

Juan, Damin and I had become good friends with Camila during our visits to Caprock.

Of course, everyone knew she was hot, except maybe her, but she was very interested in bartending and working at Gardski's with us when it opened. We'd given her updates on our progress at every visit.

And we all thought that, yes, what a blast it would be to work with her.

However, I was starting to have greater things in mind...

I had never asked her out or even hinted at any type of date or rendezvous up until this point. I had asked Josefina out the first weekend I met her and it hadn't gone too well. She hadn't said no, but she hadn't said yes either.

Now Camila and I were friends on Facebook and I had her phone number. I knew she was special and I knew there was a reason I was in Lubbock. I believed she was biggest the reason, but, I didn't feel it was relationship or sexually orientated.

It felt bigger than that, much bigger.

As I said many times "I think of her as being the lead singer in my band. And you don't mess around with the lead singer."

I needed her, but I didn't know why.

She was remarkably gorgeous in every possible way and possessed the sweetest, purest, most adventurous spirit.

She was young, Brian thought maybe 24, I guessed maybe 23. Then we agreed. "Who cares how old she is! She's behind the bar pouring us beers!"

"We're locked out!" Damin said.

Two days before Halloween, the Williams stopped construction, locked up Gardski's and closed the restaurant.

They had run out of money and filed a lawsuit with the landlord, Mr. Skibell, for all the additional time and money it was costing caused by the unforeseen damage to the building.

This had been an ongoing issue ever since the damage was discovered. The landlord covered the extra structural costs but there were many other issues at stake between the parties.

Ronald saw it coming months before, packed his tools and went back to Afton.

We were out of work.

"Do you remember that blonde haired lady that came into the restaurant from Abbeville Dental?" said Damin.

I did. There were several people who came in and out of Gardski's during the construction who had projects of their own and were looking for a contractor. And Damin was always on the lookout to sell.

"She gave me her business card," he said.

Within days we were remodeling the blonde lady's dental office that was located in a small mall, near Caprock Café.

Abbeville Dental's business was booming and they were expanding. We painted, added new cabinets and shelving in the lab where impressions, corrective devices and teeth were made. We installed a compressor, air and gas lines in the ceilings and walls, to service new dental chairs.

I had unfinished work of my own. I had written the songs Deja Vu and Love Tornado three years earlier in Tacoma. Both songs had been inspired by Josefina.

I my mind, I had confirmed that the sequel to The Secret Beast would be titled Doppelganger. Those two songs were going to be the first songs of the soundtrack.

I only had demo recordings of the songs. I wanted pro recordings.

James Robinson, aka Jdrums, lived in Miami, Oklahoma. James and I recorded and released our Deadman's Island album in 2007. At that time, I was writing and recording songs and needed them professionally produced. We met online. I was living in Gig Harbor, WA and he lived in Hollywood, CA.

I would send him MP3's of my guitar and vocal tracks that were recorded to the beat of digital drum tracks. He took my tracks and added live bass and drums from his John Bonham style drum kit, and mixed and mastered the songs.

We never met in person during our year working together. It wasn't until a random, magical moment in our future that we would meet.

The first and only time we had ever met each other in person was at the Swinging Doors Saloon in Nashville, Tennessee on November 7th, 2014, exactly seven years after our Deadman's Island album was released on iTunes, on Nov. 7th 2007. It was a social get together.

He had since moved from Hollywood back to his hometown in Oklahoma.

I called him and brought him up to speed with my plans. I wanted to drive through Tornado Alley and up to Miami and lay down tracks for Deja Vu at his Record Shack and hire him to produce the song.

On Thanksgiving Day, I made the eight hour drive from Lubbock to Miami, OK.

"I'm going to El Corazon," says the voice with a heavy, male Indian accent from the backseat.

The sun is shining as I pull into the El Corazon parking lot. "Pearl Jam's first five shows were performed here. I have waited years to visit this venue, the home of grunge!" the hitchhiker says.

"Would you like to see Eddie's home?" I ask.

"What! You know where Eddie Vedder lives?!" he says.

"Yes." I say.

"Please take me there! I will pay you money and buy you beers! he says.

"Where does your love for Pearl Jam come from?" I ask.

"I own an entertainment company in India. I promote large festivals and concerts. It is my dream to bring Pearl Jam to India!"

I drive past Endolyne Joe's Restaurant and take a right on Brace Point Drive. I drive slowly down the windy sloped road that ends at the beach.

"He lives right there, the house on the right. Let's go walk on the beach and I will take a photo of you standing in front of the lead singer of Pearl Jam's home." I say.

"This is the happiest, best day of my life!" he screams.

I woke and popped up from my reclined front seat. I had pulled off I-44 near Tulsa for a quick refresher nap.

"Hmm, that dream was just too real," I thought.

My excitement for music matched the excitement in the dream, as I drove closer and closer to Miami.

A big, tall, black haired bearded man, wearing a black top hat, with a bright green, two inch ribbon around it, and a black sleeveless t-shirt that exposed a tattooed arm, stood outside a small farm house as I drove up. It was James.

"Welcome!" he said with a smile. "Let me show you

the Record Shack."

I grabbed my electric guitar, backpack and followed him inside.

I put my gear down and stood in amazement, gazing around the Record Shack. A monster purple drum kit sat on a stage surrounded by a room full of collectibles, artifacts and treasures related to the music entertainment business.

The room looked like a small museum and had a large custom built sign that said "The Record Shack" mounted above the stage. There was unique lighting rigged everywhere for special effects.

James worked on a crew that made music videos for the likes of Gwen Stefani etc. while in Hollywood. I could see his talents displayed throughout the room. He had chairs, candles, pillows, books and rare musical instrument pieces carefully placed maximizing their appeal.

"The Record Shack is incredible bro, the energy has this fantasy vibe going on," I said.

"The Record Shack has been waiting for you. This is all here, ready for the day that you would arrive," said James.

I plugged in my guitar and for the first time ever, we played our music live, together. We played Frosty Glass, the first song we ever recorded.

For the next three days we had fun. We didn't work on Deja Vu. Instead, we filmed a music video on my iPhone 6 of us performing Frosty Glass in the Record Shack.

We filmed, edited and finished the video in three days using a free, cheesy little app on the little iPhone screen while we nipped at whiskey and collaborated with flower.

It was a blast.

The first vision board that I had ever created for my dream was in 2008. It was a collage. I put the castle, the Lamborghini and a tour bus with the Jdrums logo, and the Deadman's Island CD photo-shopped onto the side of the bus, on that vison board.

James and I finally played together.

At one point in the song Frosty Glass, the lyrics say "her eyes reflect the depth of the lies."

During the editing portion, James mentioned the idea of using a video clip of a woman with beautiful eyes in this section.

"I know exactly who could fill that part. Too bad she's not here," I said.

I was thinking of Camila's enchanting eyes.

CHAPTER 5

For the next few days, I couldn't get the video and the idea of Camila's eyes out of my head. I didn't get music for Doppelganger on my trip to the Record Shack, but I got even more, I got a manifestation, an episode for Doppelganger.

Playing live with Jdrums was a piece of my dream coming true.

What piece comes next?

Juan and I had just finished work. He threw out the idea to have beers at Caprock, but I wasn't up to it, so I said "later" in the parking lot at Abbeville Dental and we went our separate ways.

On the way back to my house, I received another nudge from the universe. I changed my mind and decided to go solo to the Caprock.

Camila was working, and I had a few Shiners.

An impulse came to me.

"Do you want to be in my movie?" I asked. "I need an actress."

"Sure! But I don't know if I'll be very good," she said.

I was in shock. First, because I didn't have a movie, and second, her answer was yes!

"Cool, I'll stop by later this week with details. You'll do great," I said.

What movie? What do I do now?

I needed a plan, quickly. She'd said "yes" without hesitation. Momentum was building fast.

Now that Camila was on board, and the reality of creating something with her was settling in, I thought anything was possible.

Expansion within days. One day I'm painting walls in a dental lab, the next I'm planning a movie scene with a west Texas, real life, Latina princess.

The idea came to have my encounter with Jdrums be episode 1 of Doppelganger. Each episode would be another piece of my dream manifesting. I wanted to create episode 2.

I received another idea…create a scene from my dream from the book The Secret Beast.

I need a red Lamborghini.

I had been pricing Lambos. It would cost me $4400 a month to lease a red 2008 LP640 Murcielago from Driving Emotions, a West Palm Beach exotic car dealer. This included insurance.

Three years earlier I had been a server in Maui and flubbed my presentation serving a bottle of wine to a couple of snooty guests. It was my first time ever opening and serving wine at a table.

I couldn't get the point of the corkscrew into the top of the cork. It kept slipping off the top and stabbing my hand.

The woman had to tell me that the wine bottle had a screw cap, not a cork. It was very embarrassing, to say the least.

Unworthiness.

I promised myself that one day that table will be turned.

I will pull up to the valet at a five-star restaurant, driving a red Lamborghini with the most beautiful woman on the planet sitting next to me. We will be treated like royalty while we dine and drink the finest of wines.

Worthiness.

$4400 a month…then what? I just want it for a day.

I checked exotic car rental agencies in Texas. I couldn't find any in Lubbock, Dallas or Austin. The cars that were available in those cities were trucked in from Houston. I googled exotic car rentals in Houston and found Auto Exotic Rentals.

I went to their website and scrolled through their inventory. They had a red Lambo for rent by the day.

They had weekday specials. If I rented the car on a Monday-Thursday by 9:00 a.m. and have it back by 4:00 p.m., it would cost $800 a day.

That's only $115 an hour! I was ecstatic.

Houston was an eight hour drive from Lubbock. The brand new plan was to leave Lubbock on a Sunday morning, drive to Houston, stay at a hotel and rent the car at 9:00 a.m. Monday morning. We could film in Houston until the afternoon, return the Lambo and then drive back to Lubbock.

Where, what, how to film, and other specific details,

would fill themselves in along the way.

I had the girl, I had the car. I was on a roll.

"Okay, here's the initial plan," I told Camila. "I want to film a scene where I take you to a five-star restaurant in a red Lamborghini. It's a classy scene. I'm wearing a black suit and tie and you're wearing a little black dress. We pull up to the valet, he takes the car and I escort you to our table. We dine and drink the finest wine," I said. "It's a scene for a book I'm writing, which is my screenplay for a movie."

"I like wine!" Camila said enthusiastically.

"That's the spirit!" I said.

I showed her the picture of the car I had on my phone and ordered another Shiner.

"Here's the catch. The car is in Houston so we need to travel there to film the scene. We'll leave Sunday and come back Monday night. I'll pay all your expenses and a hotel room for you and a friend. Damin and I'll also get a room. He'll shoot the whole episode," I said.

"I'll pay you for two days work. How about $200 a day…$400 total?" I asked.

"Sure!" she said.

I handed her four $100 bills and thanked her.

"But I get to drive the Lamborghini!" she said with excitement.

It was mid-December. I went online with Auto Exotic, and reserved it for Monday at 9 a.m. in late January. This would give me time to work out the details and get the money to fund the whole project.

It was time to create the book cover. I contacted Brenna in Seattle, my graphic artist. After telling her about Doppelganger, she came up with an idea for the cover.

"I need you to walk by yourself in a forest. I want a photo of you walking in one direction looking off to the right as you pass yourself walking in the opposite direction. So you need to take two photos for me, one in each direction. I will blend them seamlessly together. No smiling. I want a confident look on your face," she said.

Early on New Year's day, I grabbed my iPhone and went to the park. There was an inch of snow on the ground. There was no forest in Lubbock.

I duct taped my iPhone to a tree branch and touched "record video." Then I walked back and forth through the park towards the camera, and away from the camera.

I took some screen shots and Brenna did the rest.

My book, and my dream, were coming alive.

———————————

"Did you get a check today? I said.

"No, they said they mailed it three days ago," said Damin.

Abbeville Dental kept us very busy but getting paid was a little unpredictable because of the severe winter. Snow and ice had closed airports, UPS, FedEx and USPS for prolonged periods of time throughout January. Their corporate office was in Louisville, KY.

With so many closures happening at different times, tracking a simple check seemed impossible.

I didn't receive a paycheck in time to hold the Lamborghini or the hotel rooms and had to cancel the project.

Texting Camila and telling her the project was scrapped because of lack of funds made me feel sad. I thought my shot to make this happen with her was gone, until I got her reply.

"It's okay, there must be a reason why this happened, we can reschedule," she texted.

Who is this person? She was wise beyond her years.

Damin and I eventually received our paychecks and continued working with Abbeville.

"They want us to paint their whole office in Brownwood. They also want us to run gas, air and install another dental chair in one of the rooms," said Damin.

Brownwood was a small town four hours south of Lubbock, exactly half way to Houston.

"I added travel time, hotel costs and a food allowance and they jumped all over it!" laughed Damin.

We were back in business.

I had kept in contact with Auto Exotic and they were super easy to deal with.

I reserved the car for March 13th. They didn't want a deposit and said "Y'all just pay for it when you get here, we'll hold it for ya."

We were going to be in Brownwood for two to three weeks. I thought once we got the job underway we could take a trip to Houston to check out the Lambo, find hotel rooms and scout restaurants for a location to shoot.

It was late February in Brownwood and the weather was gorgeous, mid 70's and sunny every day.

We worked at the dental clinic all day, alongside several darling hygienists. It was a pleasant atmosphere. A dozen ladies with Texas accents, with me, Juan and Damin.

I had business cards made. They displayed the cover artwork for my books, my phone number and social media links. I handed them out to the ladies. I almost sold a couple copies of The Secret Beast.

After work we would go to Chili's for happy hour, and usually end up at Los Cazadores, or Humphrey Pete's, before we crashed at La Quinta.

———————————

"What are you reading?" I asked.

One of the bartenders at Humphrey Pete's was named Molly. She was real friendly and enjoyed it when Juan, Damin and I came in for beers. She loved listening to our adventures.

One night, she served us cold, frosty schooners of beer, then went and sat at a stool at the bar where she was reading a book.

"Oh just a book for school," she replied.

"School?" I asked.

"I take classes at Howard Payne," she said.

"Are you almost finished with college?" asked Damin.

"No," she laughed. "I'm only 19. I'm a sophomore."

I was a totally confused.

"How can you be only 19 years old if you are bartending?" I asked Molly.

"You only have to be 18 to bartend in Texas," she said.

Instantly, I felt a bolt of energy ripple through my solar plexus.

"Holy shit!" I said. "Then Camila may not even be 21!"

"So what?" said Damin.

———————————

Damin and I made the four hour trip from Brownwood to Houston on a weekday morning to scout the city for our project.

We went to Auto Exotic, previewed, sat in the 2013 red Lamborghini Performante, and started it up.

It was an exotic convertible, with black wheels and black stripes. It came equipped with paddle shifters mounted on the steering wheel that let the driver shift manually into another gear with a flip of the wrist. It would take a little getting used to.

We searched the area near Auto Exotics for a five-star restaurant with valet parking. We didn't have any luck, and retired to an Irish Pub for a beer.

Then it came to me. *Why look for a restaurant when a five-star hotel would have everything we need? Rooms, restaurant and valet parking.*

I did a local search and found Hotel Granduca. It had a restaurant named "Ristorante Cavour." The restaurant was rated "Best Italian" in Houston.

We quickly drove a few short blocks and there we found the incredible stucco and pastel orange colored building, Hotel Granduca.

At its entrance, a giant metal statue of a war horse being ridden by a fearless Italian General stood near the fountains and colorful gardens that were in full bloom with hot pink, white and lavender perennials.

The valet was brilliant. It operated on the veranda of the hotel in front of Ristorante Cavour.

Just inside the hotel, there was a beautiful, spacious upscale bar with a grand piano where a musician was playing "New York, New York."

Several imposing knights in suits of armor stood scattered throughout the main floor. Photo after photo of the ancient cities in Italia: Roma, Napoli, Sicilia, Venezia and Firenze, hung on the walls next to ancient steel swords, shields and battle axes. Arrangements, abundant with fresh flowers, warmed the interior.

Everything was Italian, including the Lamborghini.

It was incredible.

It was perfect!

I reserved two double rooms for Sunday night, March 12th.

JEFFREY DULLUM

CHAPTER 6

It was a sunny and breezy Sunday afternoon, March 5th.

We had three more days and our job in Brownwood would be finished. We planned to drive back to Lubbock on Wednesday. The following Sunday we would be in Houston.

"Let's go out to Lake Brownwood," said Damin.

"Where's that?" I asked.

"It's about an hour away, I want to check out the lake." he said.

"You and Juan go ahead, I'm going for a walk, and then chill in the room, and maybe grab a nap," I said.

Two hours later I received a text from Damin with a picture of a giant castle in the desert. A caption read "This is what you're missing!"

Of course! Why wouldn't there be a giant castle in the middle of the desert near Brownwood?

Two days later after work, we went to find the castle.

I had brought my black Doppelganger suit to Brownwood. It was the same suit I used for the book cover pics and the one I was going to wear in Houston when we filmed.

I brought the suit to Brownwood because I sensed I might need it.

I was right.

I jumped into the backseat of Damin's Honda Passport with the suit on a hanger. We started out of the La Quinta parking lot to head toward Lake Brownwood.

"Stop!" I said, just as we were about to merge onto the street from the parking lot. "Back up, back up, I need a red rose."

Earlier in the week I'd seen a single, beautiful, blooming red rose on a bush outside the hotel. There was only one. I noticed it because I thought if I needed a rose in an emergency, I would know exactly where to get one.

This was an emergency.

I hopped out of the car and pulled out my utility knife from my work shorts. I ran to the rose bush, sliced the stem, and stole the single red rose.

"Let's go!" I said.

I reached into the cooler in the back of the Passport and grabbed a plastic bottle of water. I opened the bottle, drank half the water, then cut two inches off the top of the bottle with my knife. I made a vase for the rose.

"I gotta say, I don't know exactly how to get to the castle. The picture I sent you was taken from a distance. All the roads around the lake look like they either circle back to the main road or dead end. I'm not sure how close we can get to it," said Damin.

We kept going in and out of range of Google Maps and it didn't show the castle.

There has to be a way.

As we got close to Lake Brownwood we could see the castle. We could see it, but we could have easily been five miles away. As we drove closer, the castle appeared and disappeared as it danced and teased us from behind the twisting, rolling landscape and scattered trees.

"That might be where it's at," Damin said, and pointed towards a large sign for a development that was mounted above a monster sized security gate.

There were no houses in view beyond the gate. But a billboard just outside the gate showed all the parcels that were for sale on a lake.

The billboard had a phone number printed below the words "LOTS FOR SALE!"

We left the gated property, and drove on a gravel road around the lake in search of anything that resembled a road that would lead us to the castle.

We could still see the castle but had no luck. There was no road.

I started to think Damin was right with his earlier hunch at the billboard. That place had to be where the castle was located.

"Let's stop by the gate one more time on our way back. I have an idea," I said.

We pulled up to the gate and stopped.

"Hold on," I said to Juan and Damin.

I called the phone number on the billboard.

"Hello, this is Jim," said a pleasant voiced man with a deep Texas accent.

"Hi Jim, my name is Jeff," I started. "I'm from the Seattle, Washington area and I'm in Brownwood this week for work. I've been looking for a piece of property on Lake Brownwood and saw your sign. I'm trying to take a look at the lots and get some pricing. Do you know who I could contact for this type of information?"

"Hi Jeff, sure, I own the properties with my brother who lives upstate. I live fifteen minutes away and could meet you there any time this week. I can't tonight, I'm heading out the door right now," he said.

"That sounds great Jim. In the meantime is there any way I could just drive through and take a peak tonight on my way back to Brownwood? The gate is locked and I noticed there was no security guard there tonight. Is there another way in?" I asked.

"Oh, just use the keypad. Here, write down this code "star 12221 pound," he said.

"Okay, star 12221 pound. Thank you Jim, I'll be in contact with you," I said, rapidly pumping my fist.

"Oh, one more thing Jeff, when you drive through you can't help but notice my brother's creation - it's an actual castle. We don't know why he wanted to build a castle on this property. It makes it a little intimidating for some folks and honestly, a little tough to sell the lots. The castle is vacant as we speak and he only comes down a couple times a year to stay in it. Once you pass the castle, the homes are just regular. I just thought you should know," Jim said.

I felt like Robin Hood as we charged the castle that

loomed into view as soon as we took the first turn in the road.

"Here's my phone," I said, as I tossed it to Damin while I quickly changed into my Doppelganger suit in the back seat.

"Juan, look out for cars, yell if you see one!" I said.

Juan smiled. "I know what to do."

The castle was enormous. It was built from large sandy colored stone blocks. It boasted several turrets, entrances, and a dozen garage doors, with sidewalks leading everywhere.

I peeked through the side door and saw furniture inside. The castle looked brand new. There were no window coverings and the grounds hadn't been landscaped.

There was no one around except the three of us.

The sky was blue and crystal clear. The stars were illuminated throughout the cosmos as the yellow sun began to set.

"I want you on the door step. Pretend you're walking out the front entrance towards me. You are leaving your castle on your way to pick up Camila in the Lamborghini," directed Damin.

As I approached the front doors, I turned and sprinted back towards the Honda to get the red rose.

"Hold on! I have to get the rose. I leave the castle with a rose and give it to her when I pick her up…the Doppelganger has style!" I yelled.

For the next fifteen minutes we scurried around the outside of the castle taking still photos and video.

"I got it, I got everything. Let's go!" laughed Damin.

We jumped back into the rig, cracked open three beers from the cooler, toasted and cheered our success as we exited through the main gate and drove back to Brownwood.

"So the check from Abbeville has been sent?" I asked Damin.

Abbeville Dental had received, signed off and approved the final invoice from our work in Brownwood. We needed this final check for Houston.

"Yep. The check is in the mail and should be waiting for us when we get back to Lubbock," said Damin.

We finished work early Wednesday and left Brownwood.

On the way back to Lubbock, I got the idea to use the material from the castle towards making a music video for the song Deja Vu, which I would call "Doppelganger: Episode 2."

This is where the part of the dream of me leaving the castle, and taking a beautiful girl to a five-star restaurant in a Lamborghini, manifests.

"Doppelganger: Episode 1," would be the live music performance with Jdrums, in the form of the Frosty Glass music video, that manifested.

Each episode would be another manifestation of my dream. My Doppelganger would be experiencing those manifestations.

I needed a photo of Camila holding the same rose that I had in Brownwood for the Deja Vu music video.

I texted Camila. "I will pay you $100 to take a photo of yourself with a special rose that I have. We just left Brownwood and I can meet you in a couple hours with the money and the rose. Just take a selfie with the rose and send it to me when you get a chance. Thank you!"

"Ok, but you take the photo. I'll be at my house, just stop by. I'll show you the black dress that I'll be wearing in Houston," she texted back.

She texted me her address and I went to her house near campus. She invited me in. Her place was a nice spacious studio with hardwood floors. A queen size bed with a white ruffled comforter sat in the middle of the room. The doors and windows were trimmed with white painted wood.

I felt awkward being in her home. Up until this point, I had only seen her behind the bar and one time at Capital Pizza where we met for a brief run-down of the project. And now I was in her home taking photos of her holding a red rose that I had given her.

"This is my dress," she said as she held up a hanger with a thin piece of black fabric hanging from it. "I'll go put it on."

Within minutes she came back from the bathroom wearing the dress. She looked absolutely stunning.

"Will you zip up the back?" she said as she walked up and turned her back to me.

I watched her naked back disappear as I pulled the zipper up to her neckline.

This has to be the most trusting person I have ever met. I took photos of her holding the rose, while telling her the story of the Lake Brownwood castle.

———————

"The accountant at Abbeville just called me and said they made a mistake, the check has not been sent yet," said Damin.

"I also think they're overpaying us a few thousand dollars. The check they're sending is a lot more than I thought! I'll have them overnight it," he said.

"Where is the check?" I asked.

"It's in Louisville," he said.

I entered Louisville, KY into Google Maps on my phone. It was a sixteen hour drive from Lubbock.

"I'm going to go get the check, especially if it's as fat as they say it is. I can be at their office in Louisville tomorrow before lunch. We have to get that check," I said.

"Really? Okay, I'll call her back and tell her to hold the check and that you'll be there tomorrow. Keep your gas receipts," he said.

It was Thursday afternoon. I grabbed my backpack and took off.

There were two main routes to Louisville, one that headed north, then east through Oklahoma and Missouri, and one that headed east, then north through Dallas and Nashville.

I could be in Nashville the next morning which was only two and a half hours from Louisville. I chose that route.

As I approached Memphis, a few hours from Nashville, I picked up a hitchhiker.

A very attractive woman in her mid-thirties slips into the front passenger seat in my car.

She has long brown hair, is wearing red lipstick , a very short gold colored summer dress and white high heels. Her cleavage is sexy and she smells good.

"Where are you going?" I ask.

"Wherever you'll take me," she says.

"I'm headed to Nashville," I say.

"Then so am I," she says.

"I just got back into town. I have businesses in LA, New York and Vegas that I have to oversee," she says.

"Welcome home," I say.

"Thank you, but now that I'm home, I have to deal with my four boyfriends," she says.

"Four, huh?" I say.

"Yes, it's so much work juggling four guys. One is the guy with the good job and money. One is the artist-type guy, a painter slash musician who keeps me entertained. One is just the nicest guy ever, brings me candy and flowers, and will do anything for me. And one is the guy with the physical tools, the one who keeps me satisfied," she says.

"Wow," I say.

"Not sure what's more work, my businesses or my men," she says.

"What kind of business?" I ask.

"I run a private escort service," she says.

I stare straight ahead at the road with both hands on the wheel, as I feel a hand touch my shoulder.

"What about you?" she says as I feel her hand gently caress my shoulder, then squeeze my upper bicep, then travel upward to the base of my neck where she extends a finger, touches my ear and speaks very softly "Don't you have needs?"

I feel paralyzed. I can't move my hands from the wheel or my eyes from the road.

"You have a big heart, I can feel it. That's why you picked me up. I sense that you are also very passionate, and I like that in a man. So what is it, baby? What do you want?" she asks, as I feel her lips on my ear and her hand run up the inside of my leg.

———————

I sprang up in the backseat of my Focus and looked out the car window. There were eighteen wheeler semi-trucks on every side of me.

I had pulled into a Love's Truck stop, parked between trailers for safety, and slept for three hours.

What a dream. Wow, where did that come from? I drove toward Nashville.

I arrived in Nashville at 5:00 a.m. Friday morning. I was hungry and knew the perfect spot for a bite to eat.

Café Coco in Midtown is open 24 hours. It was perhaps my favorite place in Nashville. I had performed there several times at open-mics.

And there it was, the strip club Deja Vu!

My whole face burst into a smile when I realized the connection between Deja Vu and my dream.

Deja Vu is where my former roommate, Jimmy, and I, and an off duty police officer had spent time after the Seahawks beat the Broncos in the 2014 Super Bowl.

It was 3:00 a.m. Jimmy didn't tip and we got kicked out of the club, including the cop! We were there for only fifteen minutes.

I drove past Deja Vu, crossed the bridge, ordered a Café Coco famous personal pan pizza, then headed to Louisville, where I picked up the check.

By noon on Saturday, I was back in Lubbock. Damin's bank was open on Saturdays and he cashed the check.

CHAPTER 7

I left Lubbock Sunday morning on the eight hour trip to Houston. Damin had a conflict and was going to drive separately. I had to be in Houston early enough to make arrangements with Ristorante Cavour, the valet and check into our rooms at 3:00 p.m.

Camila was in New Orleans attending the BUKU music festival with friends. She planned to leave New Orleans by noon Sunday and drive six hours, with her friends, to meet us in Houston.

I arrived at Hotel Granduca in the afternoon. I paid for the two rooms and took a walk around the spacious open lobby and bar. Artwork dripped from walls everywhere. The place was as spectacular as I remembered.

I went into Ristorante Cavour to scout a private area for Camila and I to have dinner. I had to consider where Damin could get some shots with the iPhone, without disrupting the other guests.

This was an extremely upscale place, so we would have to be quick, discreet and professional. But we wanted to have fun too.

There was no one in the restaurant. It wasn't open yet, I guessed.

I went to the bar and asked the bartender when it opened for dinner.

"I'm sorry, the restaurant is closed this evening. We are only open for brunch on Sundays."

Brunch was over. No dinner.

Plan B.

I told the bartender the quick version of the story. I told him I was from Seattle and was making a film, which sounded better to me than telling him we were making a music video. I told him I needed to shoot a scene with a beautiful Latina woman and me drinking fine wine at an upscale hotel restaurant or bar. I told him I had an actress coming in from New Orleans. I asked him if we could film in the bar.

I was sure the bartender was a fine young man, but by the look on his face, he wasn't about to sign off on my request.

"Hold on, let me get someone to help you," he said, and left the room.

Within minutes, a sharply dressed gentleman wearing a suit and tie appeared at the door to the bar, approached me, extended his hand and said "Hello, I'm Oscar Solis, the general manager. You want to film a scene in our hotel?"

"Yes, unfortunately I didn't realize the restaurant was closed tonight. I have an actress coming in from New Orleans, and thought we could be in and out of here in no time, without bothering anyone."

"What's the name of the actress?" he asked.

"Camila," I answered.

"Hmm, I haven't heard of her. What is the scene about?" he asked.

"A guy creates a dream and uses his thoughts and emotions to make it come true. The dinner is part of the dream manifesting," I said.

"The Law of Attraction," he mumbled.

"Yes!" I said.

"Come back this evening and I will have everything set up for you."

"Thank you!" I said. "Also! I'm gonna have a Lamborghini here tomorrow morning. You don't mind if…"

He cut me off mid-sentence. "Of course you have a Lamborghini coming tomorrow, and yes, you can film at the valet." He smiled, turned and walked away.

Damin arrived at 6:00 p.m. We went across the street to a bar in Uptown Park, and had a beer on the patio.

We game planned, then walked back to the hotel.

As we walked into the hotel lobby I immediately saw a sign posted on the open door of a room to the left of the bar that said "Reserved for Private Party."

I looked inside. There were dark burgundy curtains tied back with heavy gold rope at its entrance. Dimmed lamps lit the room. And it had book shelves, end tables and art displayed throughout.

There was a massive oval dining table in the center of the room decorated with orange roses, and two table settings on the white linen tablecloth. Two antique chairs faced each other across the table, waiting for its two special guests.

This must be our room. I thought impressed.

Soon Camila, with her friends Raphael and Vanessa,

arrived.

I'd been told that if I wanted to get the best photos possible, I should hire a make-up artist, and perhaps, use a camera other than an iPhone.

I arranged to have a professional make-up artist go to Camila's room for a make-up session before dinner. Camila and Vanessa had fun being pampered.

Meanwhile, I changed into my Doppelganger suit in my hotel room, went downstairs and met Damin in the bar.

A new bartender had come on the floor. He was very friendly and helpful. Even though the kitchen was closed, they were going to prepare some dishes from the bar menu.

Camila, Raphael, Vanessa, Damin and I gathered in the bar.

Damin directed. "Okay, listen, I'll get you and Camila walking around the corner, then look to me as you pass that knight in shining armor that's behind you, then you escort her to her chair at the table. As you sit, Camila, I want you to look up over your left shoulder as the Doppelganger leaves you and steps around toward his chair."

"Then we're gonna bring in the wine. They'll open a bottle and serve it to you just like in your dream!" he said.

The first take at walking Camila to her chair was awkward. She looked simply incredible in her little black dress and I had never been so close to that level of beauty.

76

But once I loosened up and the pressure subsided, everything began to flow.

When not one, but two servers came to the table and presented the bottle of wine, I realized that I had, in fact, created that moment. And with a little help from my friends, anything was possible.

I felt so satisfied.

Camila and I ate, Damin filmed, we drank, he photo'd, we laughed, they served, we fed each other, we toasted.

Vanessa and Raphael watched the whole night unfold from two seats the bar.

We had a blast.

After dinner, the five of us sat on the patio by the pool and celebrated our success with more drinks from the bar.

We finalized our plans to pick the Lambo up at 9:00 a.m. the following morning and film the drive with Camila to the valet at the Ristorante Cavour.

Camila had been driving all day after forty-eight hours of festivities in New Orleans. She was exhausted. Her friends had slept all day in the back of her SUV.

It was near 10:00 p.m. when Camila went to her room. Damin, Vanessa, Raphael and I went across the street to Uptown Park.

We came upon an upscale hookah lounge. We paid $20 cover per person and we were in. It was a fantastic, balmy, spring evening. We bathed in the great vibes from the environment of the lounge, and from the fun we had created in our dinner show.

The four of us went back to the room Damin and I were staying in around 2:00 a.m. Each hotel room had two private rooms. Damin crashed in his.

"X?" Raphael said.

"X? Ecstasy? Me? I never have. But I've always been curious," I said. "You snort it?" I thought as I saw a line that looked like cocaine appear in front of me.

Like riding a bike. The line was no longer in front of me.

I wasn't concerned with sleep. I was so wired with adrenaline that I had already decided to pull an all-nighter.

The three of us sat at the round kitchen table. Raphael to my left and Vanessa to my right.

I was feeling really, really good.

Then Raphael put on a pair of magic white gloves that glowed and strobed with red, green, blue, pink and orange lights. It was like he had sparklers in his hands that danced to the rhythm of the music playing on his phone. Pure magic.

And then, I felt a hand on my right leg!

Vanessa's hand was on my leg. I was flattered.

I didn't know what to do. She was a very attractive girl.

I didn't move a muscle and kept both of my hands out in the open, in plain view on the table.

Raphael kept doing his lights.

What am I supposed to do? Her boyfriend is sitting right next to me! If I put my hand under the table, it would be obvious.

I turned to Vanessa and smiled. I didn't want to be rude and leave her hanging.

Then it hit me...*Oh my god, maybe it's a threesome!*

Whatever was going on, I couldn't participate. All I could think of was that this was Camila's friend, or at least I thought she was, and I could not blow the opportunity I had to film with the Lambo and Camila.

Girls talk.

Ah, it's a set-up! This is a test and I'm not falling for it.

What seemed like several long minutes was probably only 60 seconds until Vanessa removed her hand, left the room and went to bed.

The sun rose.

I changed back into the Doppelganger. Damin gave me a ride to Auto Exotics to pick up the car.

A few weeks prior, when Damin and I had scouted Houston, I had knocked on the door of a gorgeous mansion in Uptown Park.

The mansion had a stone circular driveway that I wanted to use to stage the pick-up of Camila with the Lamborghini on the way to the restaurant.

I'd given Marsha, who owned the mansion, one of my new, professional, author business cards and told her that I would be returning and filming with a Lamborghini and an actress.

She gladly agreed. "Yes, of course you can use my driveway," and she apologized that all her early spring flowers that were blooming would be gone when we came back in March.

As I sat in the lobby of Auto Exotics, they apologized that the red Lambo was not available yet. It was rented out the night before and had not been returned yet.

After two hours they had it cleaned and ready.

They apologized again, and said that I could keep the car overnight and return it Tuesday morning for no additional charge.

Sweat was beading down my forehead as I sat in 90 degree heat in this convertible Lambo with the top down, stalled in the middle of an intersection in Houston, on a Monday morning.

I was hot, tired and embarrassed as hell, as I tried to get the damn car in gear with the paddle shifters. Instead, I kept turning on the windshield wipers and blinkers! All of Houston was honking at the guy in a black suit driving a red Lambo.

Traffic had to go around me until I finally got the car in gear.

I drove up to the hotel and gave it a practice run through the valet. We had met the guys working the valet and they were excited to participate.

The plan was to pick up Camila, drive the few blocks to Marsha's mansion, and do the shoot of me picking up my date.

Then Damin was going to take shots of us driving down the road back towards the hotel, arriving at the restaurant, and the valet opening Camila's door, and guiding us into Ristorante Cavour.

Other than Camila's battery going dead in her rig in the morning, my trip to Auto Zone in the Lambo to get her a new battery, where I got completely drenched in sweat before we even started because I didn't think to put up the roof of the car and turn on the air conditioning, and the damaged right front wheel, things went swimmingly.

We were finished by 2:00 p.m.

Damin had booked our room for one more night. The room was our office for the day.

Raphael and Vanessa lounged at the mini bar in the room while waiting for us to finish. It was a bittersweet goodbye when they headed to South Padre Island with Camila, to continue their spring break tour.

I was thrilled with what we created together but knew that our experience was a once in a lifetime moment. That saddened me. I liked Camila a lot.

"Here's the keys brah, have fun man," I said to Damin. He took the car out for a drive while I took nap.

"Is this your handy work?" I asked Damin, as I pointed to the Lambo's right front, black rim. The rim was scratched. It had been curbed.

"No man, I didn't hit anything," he said.

"Maybe I did it, I can't remember," I laughed. "Did I tell you Camila drove the car?

"She did?!" he said.

"Yep, she drove a lot better than I did. She laughed and teased me while I kept turning on the windshield wipers instead of putting it in gear in Marsha's driveway!" I said.

The Lamborghini sat in Hotel Granduca's parking lot Monday night. Neither of us felt like taking it out, so we just had a couple beers and got some sleep.

Tuesday morning we checked out of Hotel Granduca.

"I think they may have made a mistake, I wasn't charged for the mini bar. Raphael and Vanessa emptied that thing yesterday." Damin said.

I looked at my invoice. My rooms on Sunday were not billed for the mini bar either.

There was roughly $400 worth of inventory in those fridges when they were stocked full. And we had cleaned them out.

I know we tipped very well while we were guests, but this hotel had totally spoiled us, over the top.

At first I thought they'd made a mistake, until we returned the car.

Joanna ran the office at Auto Exotics. She was very helpful and had worked with me since December when

I'd tried to arrange a date to rent the car. She was also aware of my story and excited about what I was trying to accomplish.

"The damage to the wheel is $200," Joanna said.

Wow, that's a lot less than I was expecting to pay for the wheel. "So, what is the total that I owe you?" I asked.

"$200, just $200," she confirmed with a big 'ol Texas smile.

I pulled out my wallet and gave her two $100 bills.

"Y'all remember us the next time your fixin' to rent a car!" she said as I left the office.

"They didn't charge me for renting the Lamborghini, only the damaged wheel!" I told Damin who was waiting for me in the parking lot.

As he drove us back to the hotel to pick up my Focus I said "Between Abbeville paying us more than we thought and Granduca and Auto Exotics not charging us, I would say the universe had our backs again. And I got to try ecstasy! Where do you think we should invest our savings?" I asked.

"Let's go up to Austin and drink some beer!" Damin said.

I got in my Focus, pulled out of the Hotel Granduca parking lot and followed Damin's red 71 Chevelle Super Sport to Austin, Texas.

CHAPTER 8

I pull over to the side of the road and pick up a tall man in his late thirties who is standing next to a large industrial building.

There are large stainless steel tanks standing upright in the parking lot next to a stack of wood pallets and kegs.

He is hitchhiking and needs a ride. He opens the passenger door and gets in my car. A light aroma of hops wafts over me and captivates my senses. "Hi, I'm Roger," he says.

"Do you work there Roger?" I ask.

"Actually, I am part owner. It's Georgetown Brewery. My partner Manny just returned from Denver, I'm on my way to meet him," he says.

"Manny's Pale Ale?" I ask.

"Yes," he says.

"Wow, I didn't know that beer was named after the owner. Is there one named after you? I ask.

"Roger's Pilsner," he says.

"One of our beers just won the Oscar of beers at the Great American Beer Festival in Colorado. Out of 312 entries around the country, it was voted the #1 IPA. Manny received the award," he says.

"Which beer won the award? I ask.

"Bodhizafa," said Roger.

"Hmm, I've never heard of it. What is that one named after?" I ask.

"It's named after Patrick Swayze's character in Point Break," he says.

"Really? That's one of my favorite movies," I say.

———————————

Suddenly, I woke from yet another, hitch hiker dream.

I had left Lubbock (driving to Seattle) early in the morning, crossed the northeast corner of New Mexico and found my stash buried at the foot of the guardrail on I-25 after entering Colorado.

I smoked a bowl, drove north through Denver, then took a nap in my car near the Budweiser Brewing Company in Fort Collins.

After our night in Austin, Damin and I returned to Lubbock. I had begun putting together Doppelganger: Episode 2, a music video for Deja Vu on Damin's Macbook Pro.

I was editing photos and film from the castle, the rose, the dinner, the Lamborghini etc. to a track of the song Deja Vu that Alicia's brother Paul had mixed for me, when the Macbook Pro laptop crashed.

And I had no work.

My nephew Brett was working construction in Seattle. His boss needed his house reroofed.

So Juan took over my room in Brian's house.

I said goodbye to my wonderful friends in Texas and

followed the work.

Brett was also working on a rental home in West Seattle whose owner was a single lady named Linda. She was about to put her house on the market.

En route from Texas to Washington, as I was driving, I made arrangements with Linda to live month to month in her house until it sold.

Linda wanted me to paint the interior, the decks and railings at her house in exchange for rent. The house was in an incredible location. It was across the street from Lincoln Park, which was a huge wooded park with many trails just a few blocks from the beach.

It was April. Within the blink of an eye I had gone from living in West Texas to West Seattle, Washington.

I felt great, invincible, like anything that I focused on would somehow find its way through the cracks of the cosmos into my reality.

I noticed the path of this energy source flowed through people into my experience: Damin, Camila, Alicia, Brett and on and on and on, from Jim at the real estate billboard, to Oscar the GM of Hotel Granduca.

Countless, wonderful people, all lined up, playing their roles to perfection as I wandered through my dream, watching it all unfold.

I walked a half mile from my rental near Lincoln Park to California Ave. Southwest, the main retail hang-out for West Seattle.

I saw a bar called The Beveridge Place Pub and walked in.

I stood in line at the bar and waited my turn. I read a notice on a chalkboard that said "Micro Monday, Local Beers $3!"

It was Monday.

"I'll take a Bodhi," said the guy in front me. "Me too," said his friend.

"Two Bodhi's!" confirmed the bartender as he turned and poured the beers.

Bodhi? Is that what they just said?

It was my turn. I looked up to the menu board and pointed to the beer at the top titled Bodhizafa IPA.

"What's that one?" I asked.

"That's Bodhizafa from Georgetown," the bartender replied. "Bodhi what?" He said the name so fast I couldn't understand him.

"We call it Bodhi, our biggest seller by far. The name is from Patrick Swayze's character in Point Break. Georgetown Brewery is our neighbor, just down the road," he said.

I ordered a Bodhi.

As I drank the beer, I felt an incredibly strong sensation of deja vu.

Why does it feel like I've been here before? The name "Bodhi" sounded so familiar,

What does that name mean? I googled it. It read, Bodhi meaning: "wakefulness, awareness."

I fell in love with the name, the meaning of the name and the taste of the beer.

———————————

Now in West Seattle, I felt there was a lot momentum building toward my dream. I became more aware "in the moment" and watched for impulses and clues that would guide me to my next excellent adventure.

A European friend of mine posted photos on Facebook of his trip to Ponza Island with his girlfriend. Ponza is south of Rome off the southwest coast of Italy in the Tyrrhenian Sea.

The pictures of the sea, cliffsides and architecture were stunning.

I had always wanted to go to Italy on a romantic adventure.

Then I had the thought to make Doppelganger: Episode 3 in Italy.

I opened an account on my phone for the dating app called "Tinder."

In my bio, I wrote that I was an author and that I was searching for a woman to attend an event with me in Italy. The dinner event was for a book I was writing and scheduled for September. All expenses paid.

I posted a couple photos, including a pic of Camila and me standing next to the Lamborghini.

My phone vibrated.

"It's a Match!"

"Cool," I thought.

I looked closer at my iPhone. I saw a pic of an incredible looking blonde dancing in a black bikini and wearing high heels.

Feeling as if I had just won the jackpot, or had just caught a very big fish, I stood up, pumped my fist and said "Very nice!"

I scrolled through five more photos and read the bio of a twenty-five year old model, dancer, actor who had just returned from Beijing and was living in Seattle, just five minutes from me.

"Ni Hao." I sent her a text saying "hello" in Chinese.

I couldn't believe how brilliant Tinder was, complete genius and more fun than a free slot machine.

Pictures of women pop up on the screen one at a time, one after another, like flash cards. I get to preview their pic, age, how far away they live from me, and swipe the screen left for "no" and right for "yes" if I would like to meet them.

If the same two people swipe each other to the right, it's a match and now we can text each other on the app.

Tinder users are allowed to upload six photos into their profile.

I flicked through the pictures on the model/dancers profile and was quite impressed. Professional photos of her modeling on runways, lingerie shots of her in fashion mags and pictures of her performing as a go-go dancer, all boasted a sexy, elegant, graceful, stunning, artistic, incredibly talented blonde woman.

The last line on her bio said "Let's create something together."

Her name was China.

Within five minutes, I received a text reply "Ni Hao!"

It was Tuesday and within an hour we had a date set via text.

Me: "I just got to W. Seattle two weeks ago, I've discovered a couple cool bars on California St., Talarico's and the Bang Bar, a Thai place. I'll buy you a drink when you have time. I want to hear about China. It'll be fun."

Her: "I'm down! How do you like West Seattle? There's lots of cool spots."

Me: "What time?"

Her: "How's 6:30, before it gets too cold."

Me: "Of course, let's meet at the Bang Bar for drinks, and if you want Italian, we can go next door to Talarico's."

Her: "Sounds good! I like a man with a plan!"

Me: "Ha. Tomorrow or Thursday?"

Her: "Tomorrow." Followed by two smiling, kissing emojis.

Me: "Excellent choice."

Her: "Yay, you are very handsome!" more emojis.

Her: "Is that your Lamborghini?"

Me: "Depends on which part of my book you are reading."

Her: more emojis.

———————————

The next day I arrived at the Bang Bar at 6:30, pulled up a stool in the bar and ordered an IPA. I texted China to find out what she drinks.

I sat sipping my beer, looking out the window at California Ave. This moment was the absolute leading edge, exciting, adrenaline-flowing moment that I could imagine.

I love you, Tinder.

It was her.

A tall blonde wearing a white leather jacket, black stilettos and tight black spandex leggings, walked in. I stood and went to greet her.

As the host led us to our table, with my IPA in hand, I followed China.

She had a model's legs with a dancer's figure, all high up in the air.

The felt like a rockstar as I glanced at the employees and guests in the restaurant on the way to our table. Their faces asked "Who is this guy with this incredible woman?"

I was rolling like my Doppelganger with a smile that stretched from Lincoln Park to Alki Beach.

My experience with Camila, walking through a restaurant with a gorgeous, sexy woman on my arm, had prepared me well.

Our table was tucked nicely into a corner at the back of the room.

Two chairs on either side of a small square table with a single fresh cut rose as a centerpiece, awaited us.

I felt like I was boarding a roller coaster in a theme park. We sat, fastened our seat belts, looked at each other and smiled. *Let's do this.*

I couldn't stop smiling. I looked at China. She had shoulder length straight blonde hair. She wore cherry red lipstick that blended perfectly with her white leather jacket, striking black eyelashes and porcelain skin.

There was something of a Marilyn Monroe about her stylish punk rock look...sexy...edgy...gorgeous...which totally turned me on.

I wanted her in my band.

The server brought a glass of Chardonnay as we said our fresh, awkward hellos. Small talk ensued.

We ordered dinner.

We talked about the country of China as we ate. She shared her recent stories of her time in Bejing, and I related with my time in Shanghai in 2008.

We ate.

"Dessert?" our server asked.

"No thank you," we said at the same time.

"It'd be nice to smoke a joint right now," I thought I heard her mumble.

"Huh?" I said.

"You smoke?" she asked.

The joy on her face matched the joy on mine.

We decided to go bud shopping.

"Leave your car here. I'll drive. I know the area better than you and I'm a great driver, then we'll go to my place," she said.

A woman with a plan, I loved it.

We decided to go to Bud Nation. She had never been there.

It was around 10:00 p.m. when we walked into the bud store on Roxbury St.

We showed our ID's at the door, and made our way to a long glass display case that separated the shoppers from the merchandise.

Imagine walking into a small retail space that had probably once been a shoe repair store, but was now a fireworks stand.

Sativa, edibles, grams, pipes, joints, Indica, eighths, instruction pamphlets etc. all hung proudly on the wall, waiting for someone to notice, point to them, and choose them.

"Hi, can I help you?"

I turned to China "You want a joint, right?"

"Sure!" she said.

"What kind of joint are you looking for? Are you wanting a creative high? a body high? a head high? are you wanting more energy? Want to explore space?" asked the informative Bud Nation sales team member.

As we scanned the overwhelming selection, China pointed eagerly to the joint section on the wall and said "One of those!"

"Would you like grape, strawberry, or orange?" asked the informative Bud Nation sales team member.

"Grape," she answered without hesitation. I looked at the display. The price was $25.00 each.

Wow, that flower must be powerful, like the Grand Finale on 4th of July.

I was having so much fun.

China looked at me and said softly "Should we get one for the morning?"

You know what I just heard.

"Well, well, well yes...absolutely we need one for the morning!" I said.

As she said to the informative Bud Nation sales team member "Get us a strawberry one too!" *Why not get a case to last the rest of the week?!*

We arrived at her apartment by 10:45 p.m. I met her small dog and her cat. They let me pet them and welcomed me like family.

I felt this peaceful, fun, feminine, sexy, creative and honest energy in the infinite field as I floated thru the matrix China had created in her two-bedroom apartment.

She gave me the tour of her dressing room.

The overflowing wardrobe section, pink make-up station, the shoes, accessories, the motivational affirmations tacked up on a grease board event calendar was all in harmony inside the vortex I was standing in.

China made us cranberry vodka drinks in tall glasses that had red, frozen, ice cubes in the shape of high heels.

Then she changed into very short shorts.

We sat on her couch and smoked the grape joint. Wonderfully stoned, we watched Bob's Burgers.

China stretched her beautiful long legs across my lap. I massaged her feet and worked her muscles as we laughed to the TV.

"You have an amazing touch," China said quietly.

With each lap my hands took around her legs, starting at the thighs, up to the hips, around to the quads, down to the side of her knees, to shin, to calf, to ankle, to foot, to tippy toe and then back up, I expanded the canvas I was painting on by sliding my hands closer, closer and closer to her upper inner thigh area.

It felt good. It felt right.

Soon, she spoke.

"Not on the first night" I heard her say in the most loving way.

As if a fairy godmother was saying "All of your wishes will come true in their own time young man, but tonight, tonight is not one of those times."

I grinned at China and said, "Of course."

She woke me.

"Come on, let's go to bed," she said.

It was early morning and we had fallen asleep on her couch.

I followed her into her bedroom and dropped onto the right side of her California King.

I rolled over in bed mid-morning to a sexy, comforting "good morning." She spoke with eyes closed, with her hands wrapped in the sheets snuggling her neck.

"You get to see me without makeup," she said softly.

This chick is amazing. I got up and went to the bathroom.

When I came back, I dropped right back in bed where I'd been.

She was lying on her right side with her back toward the center of the bed. I was on my left side with my back toward the center. We did not touch.

This was the moment I thought to make a little incidental contact to see if she throws a flag.

Like carefully backing up a truck into a loading dock, I put my body in slow motion reverse until our lower backs touched. Then slowly up her back until our shoulders touched.

We were back on back, sharing mutual energy, for about ten seconds.

I was grinning ear to ear at the wall in front of me as she slowly pulled out of the back mashing, in the same sweet way she had on the couch last night.

But it was when I heard her say "We still have the strawberry one left," that I fell in love.

It was around noon. We had walked her dog and began the journey back to my car that was parked on 42nd Avenue.

We exchanged phone numbers once we arrived.

She reached over from the driver's seat of her SUV, and tickled my chest and said "Thank you for being such a gentleman."

I got out of her rig. We said our goodbyes.

She smiled and drove off.

CHAPTER 9

Now that I was living in West Seattle, I texted Josefina. I hadn't heard from her in a year or two and thought I'd check in.

"You're in West Seattle? That's where I want to move to. I'm still in Tacoma," she said.

Josefina was working on her yoga certification but didn't mention if she was still bartending. Life was good. I didn't share any details of my life, where would I start?

I was happy to know she was doing well. She had set the bar high for the woman of my dream world. I felt I was on the path.

I drove south to Tacoma to put in a bid on reroofing a house, another lead from Brett.

I got the job. The owner, Matt, gave me cash up front to purchase the roofing materials. I drove to nearby Port Orchard to visit my old friend Honeycutt who managed Washington Cedar Roofing Supply.

I paid for the roofing and scheduled a delivery. On the drive back to W. Seattle, I drove through Gig Harbor, a town on the water abundant with spectacular waterfront mansions, which is between Port Orchard and Tacoma.

This is where my waterfront dream castle stood. It was called Green Gables. I had an impulse to visit the castle. It was built at the end of a small peninsula, had several hundred feet of waterfront beach, a monster deep water dock, and views of Raft Island and the

Olympic mountains.

I had visited the house once before. The result of that visit had been that I was invited to lunch, and was invited to move to Maui to live and work on the owner's farm.

Tim, the owner, had since sold the Green Gables. I had not met the new owner.

I pulled up to the driveway and the gate at the entrance was open. I drove in, parked my car, walked up to the entry and knocked on the door.

There was no answer. I placed my professional author business card at the front door with a note on the back saying "I would like to film a scene for my movie at your home. Please call if interested. Thank you!"

Two days later, while roofing the house in Tacoma, I received a phone call.

"Hello, this is Gary…I'm calling for Jeffrey?"

"Who?" I had no idea who this was.

"Somebody left their business card at my house in Gig Harbor," he said.

"Oh! Yes, that was me," I said.

"I appreciate you stopping by my house. However, I am not interested in investing in a movie at this time," he said.

"Oh no, I apologize for the misunderstanding. I am not looking for money. I'm a writer and want to create an episode using your house. I used to be your neighbor and lived right across the inlet. I have written much about the house that you now own," I explained.

"Oh, I see. I was in the movie industry for 10 years. It's a tough business, but I enjoyed it," he said. His voice relaxed. "Sure, you can do what you want here. Just stop by and arrange it with Donna. She's the caretaker and lives in the guesthouse on the right after you enter the gate," he said.

I was in happily shocked.

I drove to the property and met with Donna, who had also been the property manager for the previous owners.

Donna gave me a tour of the mansion. I had been in the house before but had never been shown the secret passageways, and spectacular hidden rooms.

It felt as if Bruce Wayne, the Batman could live here, or even the Doppelganger.

I was so excited.

As I was finishing talking with Donna, and scheduling a day to possibly shoot photos and film, the owner Gary arrived. I thanked him and asked if there was anything I could do for him.

I noticed the roof of the guesthouse needed cleaning. The guesthouse stood among a grove of tall fir trees. The roof was steep and high, and was covered with broken branches, pine cones, and needles.

"How about if I clean the roof of your guesthouse?" I asked.

"Sure, that sounds good. Arrange it with Donna. Thank you," he said.

"No, thank you!" I said.

I finished the reroof in Tacoma, then cleaned the roof at the castle guesthouse in Gig Harbor.

Green Gables was completely booked all summer long. Donna thought it would be best to film after September, once the guests were gone, the castle would be empty.

That was great for me and it would give me time to make a plan.

I wanted to go to Venice, Italy in September.

I liked the options.

I had talked to China about doing a Doppelganger episode. I had the idea of hiring her and several of her friends to party and do a film shoot on a chartered yacht.

In my original dream and on the vision board I created in 2008, along with the castle, Lamborghini, Count Gilbert/JDrums tour bus etc., I had put a photo of a large yacht moored at the sprawling, deep water dock at the Green Gables.

I had imagined my kids, friends and loved ones, loading onto the yacht, then laughing and partying while cruising the waters with my hot Latina girlfriend and me.

I wrote the song Carnival Dream about that vision.

I'm sure my kids and hot Latina girlfriend wouldn't mind if I added four or five go-go dancers in bikinis, to the dream.

"Who's your photographer?" asked China.

"Photographer? I don't really need one, do I? I was just thinking of using a tri-pod, or I'm sure my buddy Damin would love to fly up and take some shots, like we did in Houston," I said.

"What kind of camera?" she asked.

"My iPhone 6," I said.

"An iPhone 6?!" She looked shocked. "You can't use an iPhone! Start over! This needs to be done with the highest quality equipment, and I can't put my career on the line doing a shoot with an iPhone. I'm sorry, but you really need to start all over. This is why I only work with professional photographers," she said. "I also need a script, I have to have a script! I need to study my lines if I am going to do any acting. This all has to be written first," she explained.

I understood what she was saying. The whole iPhone thing, it was kind of funny.

But to watch the meltdown from her thinking that I owned a Lamborghini, to that I didn't, was remarkable. She wasn't happy.

After searching "yachts for rent in Seattle," and learning that you don't rent yachts in Seattle, you rent ferries, and after forgetting that it rains a lot in Seattle, and that yacht rentals are in Miami, Houston and the Caribbean, and after learning that they cost thousands of dollars a day to rent, I decided to focus on Italy.

Plus, she was blonde, what the hell was I thinking?

"How ya doing on finding a Latina to take to Italy?" Damin asked on the phone call from Texas.

"Ah man, I'm having fun but auditions are expensive!" I said.

"If it were me, I would just go by myself. I wouldn't drag some chick along. You'll find one when you get there," Damin advised.

I tried one more time.

"It's a Match!"

Wow, she's hot.

I looked through the photos of my new Tinder match.

She was a 100 percent Latina actress from Cleveland, Ohio. She had long black hair, had been in the Miss Ohio Latina beauty pageant, was used in a crowd scene in Fast 7. She was looking for opportunities.

Her name was Isabella. She wanted to meet at Denny's restaurant near the SeaTac International Airport.

My first thought was, *Isn't that where most of the prostitutes hang out?*

But after a few more texts, I learned she had been visiting a friend in Bremerton and had a flight back to Cleveland from Seattle that night.

She was passing time on Tinder.

It was 11:00 a.m. and I decided to make the twenty minute drive from W. Seattle to the airport and meet her.

I drove into Denny's parking lot and parked my car. I got out and started walking toward the front entrance.

There was a Hispanic girl with a small brown suitcase sitting on the curb in the shade at the edge of the parking lot near the restaurant entrance.

She stood up, looked at me and smiled.

I started walking across the parking lot towards her and smiled.

She was wearing a black spaghetti strap top and a pair of very tight yoga pants with bell bottoms. Her pants were decorated with turquoise, burgundy and gold triangles. She had a black fanny pack covered in rhinestones that hung from her left hip.

She was phenomenal.

She walked right up to me and gave me the most loving hug imaginable. I was blown away.

"Are you hungry?" I asked.

She deserved more than a meal at Denny's. We drove five minutes to the Azteca Restaurant in South Center for lunch.

As the server walked us to our table, I realized that this practice of walking with beautiful, young ladies was becoming normal for me. I loved the feeling of being in the presence of such beautiful women, who most, including myself, could only ever dream of being with. How was this happening?

We ate lunch. She still had five hours until her flight.

We drove to my place in West Seattle.

"Do you want to smoke a joint?" she asked.

We sat at my kitchen table and smoked.

"Come on, I want to show you Lincoln Park. We can walk down to the beach," I said.

As we walked through the park she said "Do you want to smoke another joint?"

We handed the joint back and forth as we descended the steep trail from the park to the beach.

As we walked, I told her my preliminary plans for Italy.

"You sure talk a lot," she said.

She was so mellow, so chill, she was amazing.

We got down to the beach and I took photos and video of her posing on driftwood for her Instagram portfolio.

Then we sat together on the driftwood.

"Do you want to smoke another joint?" she asked.

She pulled one out of her fanny pack. We passed the joint back and forth as we walked back up the trail to my house.

"I love Seattle, I love shopping for joints," she said.

We got back to my place, smoked another joint and looked at the clock.

It was time for her to go.

I drove her back to the airport, and said goodbye to Isabella.

CHAPTER 10

"You should have let me buy you the baseball cap," says the sharply dressed Italian as he speaks to his lady. While I drive, I can hear them talking in the back seat.

She is a very stylish woman.

I picked them up hitchhiking near a Sheraton Hotel. They had told me they'd attended a fundraiser at the Sheraton.

"I do not wear caps," she says with a very strong Latin accent.

"There was a Seahawks cap and a Mariners cap. You should have agreed to let me buy both of them for you," he says.

"Why would you buy something for me that I would not wear?" she says. "Why don't you wear skinny jeans?"

"The cap would be useful. Skinny jeans are not useful," he says calmly.

"A cap is not useful," she says holding her ground.

"A cap IS useful, it will keep the sun from your face when you go hiking," he says.

"But I do not go hiking," she says.

"Now you can go hiking and not to worry about the sun on your face," he says.

"I have my black hair to protect my face if I decide to go hiking," she says. "You wear skinny jeans and go hiking."

"That is not useful, skinny jeans are not useful for hiking. Skinny jeans are not useful for anything," he says.

"But I like skinny jeans on men. That is useful to me," she argues.

―――――――――――

Suddenly, I awoke while napping at Love's Truck Stop.

Dude, shut-up. She doesn't want the cap. Get the jeans.

I continued motoring my way back to Lubbock. It was late July and I planned to go to Italy in mid-September.

Damin had gotten a great interior paint job in a nice, newer, air-conditioned house in Lubbock. He had invited me to come back down to Texas to work with him.

The tall walls and high ceilings needed to be painted in a variety of different shades. All the interior woodwork had to be brushed, and all the kitchen cabinets needed to be masked and sprayed.

We first needed to remove the kitchen drawers and doors, then spray them in a spray booth inside a metal building that he and Ronald were remodeling.

I had an outstanding debt with the State of Washington for $1800.00.

It was for a few months of back child support.

A few years back, my son, the youngest of my three children, had moved back into his biological mother's house after I split to Oakland. Child support payments kicked in again for six more months, until he turned eighteen years old.

I could not renew my expired U.S. Passport and go to Italy until that outstanding debt was paid and wiped clean from my record in Washington D.C.

As I drove to Lubbock to paint, I received a text from a guy named John who had a house in Port Orchard that needed to be reroofed. John commuted to Tacoma and worked with Matt at Albertson's grocery store.

I had done Matt's roof a few months earlier in Tacoma and he had referred me to John.

I had given John a bid in early July but he'd decided to wait and get more bids. He never got back to me so I followed the work. Hence I went to paint in Lubbock.

John texted me that he'd accepted my bid and wanted me to start the job. I told him I was driving to Texas to paint for a few weeks.

He texted me back and said when I was free, he'd pay me nearly $2000.00 more than my original bid price. Evidently, the price of roofing had gone up since I had been in the business twenty years earlier.

Sold.

I painted in Lubbock for two weeks and made great money with Damin.

Then I drove back to West Seattle, commuted by ferry to Port Orchard, and started John's roof.

I called the State of Washington and talked to the powers that be. I told them I would make a cash offer to my ex-wife and pay off the debt.

"If the custodial parent accepts your offer, she needs to fax us a letter saying that this child support debt has been paid in full and that she wishes to close the account. Once that happens, then we will send that information to Washington D.C. It will take them a few weeks to clear your name. You will not know if your name has been cleared until you submit your new passport registration forms. Good luck," said the helpful state government employee."

I texted my ex-wife and made her a cash offer of $1000.00. The outstanding debt was not accruing interest and I could pay little or nothing towards it…unless of course I wanted to get my passport. I was hoping she would bite and take the quick cash.

"How about $1200.00?" she counter-offered.

"Sold!"

I met her and her husband at the Target store parking lot in Tacoma and gave her the $1200 cash.

I gave her the fax number and instructions to close the account and report that she was paid in full.

I had no guarantee she'd fax the State and clear my name. But the way things were manifesting for me, I knew I already had my renewed U.S. Passport.

Within one week, a lady from the State of Washington called me and told me they had received the fax from my ex-wife. My case was closed.

She said that she had immediately sent all the info to Washington D.C. to clear my name from the No U.S. Passport list.

Incredible.

In one moment, one single moment, I was free from a financial obligation that I had served diligently for twenty years and free to travel the world.

I filled out the passport application, and put it in an envelope along with a check and two passport photos of myself taken at Walgreen's drug store.

I addressed the envelope to the U.S. Passport Office, then went to the post office on California Avenue.

As I waited in line, I watched the postal clerk help a lady at the counter. The postal worker was an older gentleman and showed no emotion as he worked. He handed the lady a receipt for the package she was shipping and said "Next."

It was my turn.

I placed my envelope on the counter and said "I just want a stamp to mail this."

Without making any eye contact with me, the clerk took the envelope and placed it on the scale.

I am going to make this guy smile. I was extremely excited about getting my passport and I wanted my positive energy to touch this man.

I had tried this experiment at the DMV in the past, when I had gone to get my driver's license renewed. While I waited at the DMV for my number to be called, I was sending strong positive vibes throughout the room.

For ten minutes I focused like Harry Potter. Soon, people sitting in chairs, waiting their turn, started smiling as they conversed and interacted with each other.

My number was called. Every state employee smiled at me, including the lady who ran the camera for the driver's license photos. She was laughing and joking with everyone who got their picture taken, including me.

The man at the post office handed me my receipt. I looked at the receipt and saw that it cost $2.78 to mail my envelope. Even though it was only $2.78, I was a little surprised that it cost that much.

As I looked up from my receipt, the postal clerk was smiling at me like Santa Claus.

"I added insurance to your envelope, it will be there in two days," he said.

He had my back. He didn't even ask if I wanted insurance. He knew it was important to me.

It was more confirmation from the universe that everything was lining up for me to go to Italy.

The most exciting part was being aware of how it was manifesting.

Six days later I received my passport in the mail without paying the rush charge. Some might say that the speed in which it was processed was because it was late August, and applications for passports had dwindled as summer travel was ending. I knew it was more than that.

_____

My first stop would be Venice. I checked airline flights daily.

I finished John's roof in Port Orchard. His neighbor and brother-in-law, Bob Bell, lived next door and wanted me to reroof his house.

Bob Bell told me that he and John had gotten three bids each from other roofing companies for both their houses. I was thousands of dollars cheaper, even after John offered and paid more than my original bid.

I did Bob's roof.

I worked alone and drove my Focus full of tools to work as I continued commuting from West Seattle to Port Orchard.

Matt from Tacoma had let me use his compressor and I rented a coil roofing nail gun and air hoses. I had purchased a tear-off shovel, roofing jacks, knife, flat bar, knee pads etc. from Washington Cedar when I did Matt's house. The owners took care of disposing the old roofing.

_____

My plan was to go to Venice, stay at the Ca Maria Adele, find a gorgeous woman to have dinner with and then travel eighty miles to Sant'Agata Bolognese and visit the Lamborghini factory.

I was walking on Alki Beach in West Seattle, listening to an Abraham-Hicks recording on YouTube. Abraham-Hicks is a law of attraction teacher and travels the world putting on workshops. One of her guests mentioned an upcoming event in Rome. I went to the Abraham-Hicks website and looked up their schedule.

Abraham-Hicks was to have her first event ever in Italy, coming up on September 17th in Rome.

I had never been to an Abraham-Hicks conference and began looking at flights to Rome instead. I also researched the islands of Ponza and Capri. I had always heard the Amalfi Coast was very romantic. Once I saw pictures of all of these places, I made plans for Rome.

I finished Bob Bell's roof and made great money. Having put my first roof on a house when I was 10 years old, and having my own roofing business for a decade, I knew what I was doing.

Bob's mother, Mrs. Bell, lived in a separate house on the property.

"My mom needs her roof done too. I don't know if you want to do it or not, two layers need to be removed, it's steep as hell and it's two and a half stories off the ground on the backside," Bob said.

It was the first week of September. I accepted the challenge to reroof Bob's mother's house. I made $5500 cash in 7 days and saved Bob's mother a few thousand dollars on a brand new roof.

The house that I was renting from Linda in W. Seattle, had been sold. I made arrangements to move out by Sept. 15th.

I wanted one more roof job before I purchased my flight to Rome. I wanted to take plenty of money with me.

"Hey Jeff, this is Bob Bell. You did such a great job

on my mom's roof, she'd like you to reroof her detached garage," he said.

It was Monday Sept. 12th. I accepted the job for the garage reroof. But I knew if I took the job that I would miss the Abraham-Hicks show in Rome on Saturday 9/17.

I'd have to fly out of Seattle no later than early Friday morning, 9/16, if I was going to make it to the conference.

I wouldn't have the roof finished until Friday.

It was okay. I thought the Abraham-Hicks conference had been there to guide me to Rome, which it had. I pocketed another $3000 cash from the garage job, and bought a one-way ticket to Rome leaving Sunday, September 18th.

"Thank you for all the work, Bob. Because of that work, I just purchased a one-way ticket to Rome leaving this Sunday," I said.

"When are you coming back?" asked Bob.

"If I fall in love with a hot Latina, I may never!" I laughed.

JEFFREY DULLUM

CHAPTER 11

I flew from Seattle to LA, then sat in an airport bar and watched NFL games during my three and a half hour layover.

I boarded the flight from LA to Oslo, Norway. After landing in Oslo, I had an eighteen hour layover before my connecting flight to Rome the following day.

I landed at the airport just outside of Oslo. The airport was the most beautiful airport I had ever been in. The wood beam ceilings, sparkling tile floors, elegant shops and stylish uniforms worn by airlines employees gave it an expensive vibe.

I took a train from the airport to downtown Oslo.

It was dark, around 7 p.m. when I arrived downtown. I started walking, searching for the Anker Hostel. I'd booked the hostel with Wifi at the airport and had taken a screen shot of the map.

"Do you know this street?" I asked a young man on the sidewalk as I pointed to the screen shot on my phone.

"Yes! I live right next door to the hostel. Follow me!" he said. He sounded excited.

Wow, that was easy.

"You speak English!" Now I was excited.

"Not very well," he said.

"What do you mean? We are having a

conversation," I said.

"Thank you. I just finished my English class at the university. Do you want to go have beers? I will show you the city," he said.

Within minutes of landing in a foreign country at night, while searching for my hostel, or beer, whatever comes first, I meet a young Iraqi student named Wael on a city street who lives right next door to my hostel, who just got out of English class, and who offers to show me the town and drink beers.

We went to several unique, incredible bars, sampled the beers, and played pool with two Germans.

"I will show you the King's castle! Wael said.

"Shut up! you guys have a King?" I said.

"Yes, let's finish our IPA's and I will take you there. It's a short walking distance," he said.

Not only had Wael led me to the IPA's, he led me to the Royal Palace.

The public Palace grounds surrounded the castle and were covered with a fine layer of red crushed rock. Genius, the rocks crunched loudly making it impossible for any enemy to sneak up to the entrance on foot.

Dramatic lighting lit up the fortress. A giant, fifty foot statue of a war horse and rider stood proudly in the courtyard.

A soldier in uniform, carrying a rifle, paced back and forth with perfect strides at the main gate.

It was getting late when we started walking back to

the hostel.

"I must go now," Wael said, as we returned to the hostel.

And like a ghost, he was gone.

The following morning I had a complimentary breakfast at the hostel, then took a train back to the Oslo airport and caught my flight to Rome.

I landed in Rome in the afternoon and took the forty minute train ride to Roma Termini, the central railway station in downtown Rome. My plan was to stay overnight in Rome. The next morning I would take a train to Naples, and then another train to the city of Salerno.

"Do you speak English?" was the phrase of the day as I managed to navigate to the Freedom Traveler Hostel in Rome. What felt like three miles, was actually only three blocks from the train station.

I stopped at a small shop and ate my first pizza ever in Italy. It was surreal.

The Freedom Traveler served free wine and crackers on their outdoor patio every night from 7-10 p.m.

Between my new friends Chris, Glen, Julia, and two other tables of travelers we drank approx., at least, twelve bottles of red and white wine. And then, per the hostel's "Things to do in Rome!" bulletin board, we decided to go to the Yellow Bar down the street, which never closes, for live Karaoke.

The Yellow Bar was incredible, perhaps the most diverse setting that I've ever been a part of. There were people from all over the world. I could hear different languages being spoken as I explored the bar which was an international melting pot. I watched one man standing in front of me pick-pocket car keys from his friend's pocket! The thief was just practicing and laughed as he returned the keys to his friend. A drummer and guitar player were on stage and played along with anyone who wanted to sing Karaoke. They were incredible musicians. It was amazing to experience the completely packed bar sing Wonderwall and Ho Hey together in unison, at 3:00 a.m., in downtown Rome.

The next morning I took a train to Naples, then a train to Salerno.

I arrived in Salerno in the early afternoon. I left the train station and started searching for the Kione Hostel.

"Hello sir," do you know this hostel? I said slowly while pointing at my phone.

"Kione Hostel?! Yes, follow me!" he said.

Wow, that was easy.

Eduardo, a native of Salerno, spoke very good English. He walked very fast as we talked.

"What brings you to Salerno?" he asked.

"I'm writing a book," I said. "Do you know any photographers?"

What I had learned from my time with China, is that if you want to get a hot model for an event, go through a photographer.

"Jeff! I have a friend who is a photographer but she

is out of town," he said. "Jeff, here is the hostel, I must go now and will see you again!" he said and hurried off down the sidewalk.

I checked into the Kione hostel, which looked as if it could have been a school in the past. It had spacious hallways, rooms and tile floors. Each room had up to ten beds. There was a large community room with sofas, tables and chairs, a TV and a coffee vending machine. Some guests were not guests, and had stayed there for months. For $9 a day, I thought I might join them.

I walked a block up the street to the In Time café bar.

It was late afternoon, and I was the only customer inside the bar. There were five locals, all Italian men, that were chilling on the patio outside, smoking and staring at me.

I approached the counter at the bar and looked up at the menu on the wall, then at the barista.

"Mocha?" I asked the barista. I could not see any word that resembled "chocolate" on the board.

She didn't understand English.

The Italian woman in her late twenties was absolutely stunning. She had short black hair, an exotic face and a very inviting smile. She wore tight denim jeans.

I had never experienced a language barrier with a beautiful woman before.

Oh my god, this is going to be a fun order.

Back and forth, we tried to communicate.

Finally, one of the men on the patio came in and went behind the bar. I learned later that he was the owner, and he spoke a little English.

With his help, I finished ordering, then dumped my euro coins on the counter. I hadn't had time to memorize what they were worth, and I was not going to break out my reading glasses.

The mocha cost 1.20 euros.

What I had learned from Wael in Norway, and from the bartenders at the Yellow Bar, was that tipping 20% in Europe is a lot.

After she picked up the 1.20 euros from the counter, I tipped her another euro. Her name was Teresa. She smiled.

I sat outside on the patio at table near the other four men. They introduced themselves to me. They were very friendly.

Rocco, Nicholai, Fabio could not speak a word of English but Michaela could speak enough to translate. Soon, I also met Roberto, Vito, Ettore and Maximillian or Max who introduced himself as the owner.

The following morning, I woke up and walked next door to In Time for espresso.

Just the sight of Teresa working behind the counter provided more energy than any shot of espresso on the menu board.

I used Google translate on my iPhone and found "same as yesterday!" in Italian to order my espresso.

Then I stood outside on the patio next to a tall bistro table in the spectacular morning sun and waited for my mocha.

Teresa brought my drink out to me. I noticed her long, black hair shimmering in the sunlight as it extended all the way down her back. She was wearing a baseball cap.

I felt a rush of deja vu. *Why does this feel so familiar?*

The brim of her cap shaded her face from the sun as she placed the cup, saucer and spoon on the table in front of me. She smiled, glanced down at my bare legs and feet, turned and walked back into the bar. I was wearing board shorts, flip flops and a t-shirt.

Did she just check me out?

I had an impulse. I looked around at the other customers on the patio and inside the bar and noticed that I was the only person wearing shorts. Everyone else was wearing long skinny jeans.

Even people walking past the bar outside wore skinny jeans. Everywhere I looked, everyone was dressed fashionably in tight fitting collared shirts, colorful shoes and skinny jeans.

Compared to my surroundings, I was dressed like a complete slob.

Then deja vu struck again. I was dazed, frozen in a moment of time. I sensed strongly that I had experienced this before.

I finished my espresso, waved goodbye to Teresa at the bar and planned to go clothes shopping. *How can I meet a beautiful Latina dressed like a slob?*

Salerno is on the eastern shore of the Tyrrhenian Sea. It is located at the gulf, the east side of the peninsula, at the beginning of what is referred to as the Amalfi Coast.

The Kione Hostel was only a half a mile from the sea. There was a boardwalk along the shore that stretched for a two miles. The city streets ran parallel with the beach.

The beach area was pleasantly clean and populated with walkers, tourists, street vendors and police. I could see a carnival at one end of the beach, and restaurants, kiosks and bars stretching out in the other direction.

Two blocks off the beach was a street called Corso Vittorio Emanuele. The wide street was an outside mall with retail stores, gift shops, restaurants and bars standing on both sides. Shoppers, tourists and party goers filled the street that stretched for several blocks.

There were outdoor patios in front of the restaurants and bars that made it an epic scene for beer, wine and people watching.

At one end of Corso Vittorio Emanuele Street was the train station that I arrived at. At the other end of the street, were old, narrow cobblestone alleys and walkways, atypical of what one might have come to know from pictures of Italy. The thin alleys weaved through churches, apartments, hotels and older shops.

The street between Corso Vittorio and the beach was the financial district.

I walked into one of these banks. "Dollars for euros?" I said, as I showed the bank teller my American dollars.

"No," she said and pointed across the street.

"Go to that bank?" I confirmed as I pointed in the same direction.

For two hours I tried to find a bank where I could exchange my dollars. Each bank teller said that they didn't exchange, and would point me to another bank across the street.

"Pastaffa!" said another teller, and he pointed across the street. He was certain I would find what I was looking for there.

"Pastaffa?" I asked.

I'm not hungry, does he think I'm looking for food? What is pastaffa? I don't see anything that looks like a restaurant...is he saying pasta?

"Si! Pastaffa! Pastaffa! he said again and again as he kept pointing across the street.

I walked across the street, directly to the spot he'd pointed to. I didn't see a restaurant or a bank.

All I saw was a post office. I walked inside, went up to the counter and asked the lady "US dollars, exchange to euros?"

"Yes, I can help you with that!" she said in perfect English.

"Excellent!" I said.

Then it occurred to me, the gentleman saying "pastaffa" was saying "Post Office."

Here I was in a foreign country, attempting what? Attempting to find a photographer and a beautiful Latina? To do what? I'd been lucky enough to find the correct trains to get to Salerno, and get directions to the hostel without knowing more than a few words of Italian.

How was I going to communicate anything more complicated? like what I wanted to do for my book? I was having difficulty just ordering coffee and getting euros!

I walked back to Corso Vittorio street. I knew what I needed. I needed Italian skinny jeans.

I saw a few American store fronts, The Gap, Banana Republic and a Burger King. The rest were spectacular, strange and new.

Then I had one of the greatest moments of magic or coincidence I could have possibly imagined in the quest of my dream, and there had been several moments like this along the way.

From meeting Josefina six years earlier in Tacoma then her double, her doppelganger Camila, to the castle at Lake Brownwood, to money always appearing at the right time, to getting my passport in record time, to the right person always appearing out of nowhere at the precise moment I needed them, this moment topped them all.

I saw a Doppelganger Men's Store.

Is this even freaking real?!

I bought navy skinny jeans. I bought white skinny jeans. I bought denim skinny jeans. I bought white shoes. I bought grey shoes. I bought ocean blue, dark grey and off-white collared shirts. I bought two sport jackets, a tie and a belt. I bought white footies to wear with my white shoes.

I showed off my professional author business card with the Doppelganger book cover on it to the store employees. I took photos of the store and selfies with the store's tailor, Giovanni.

I shopped like a doppelganger, at the upscale Doppelganger Men's Store.

I left the store feeling like I had just won the lotto.

And if that wasn't enough.

As I walked, just a few doors down from the Doppelganger store, I saw a women's fashion store named "Deja vu!"

On the store's front window "Deja" was spelled in large black bold letters outlined with thick white lines. "Vu" was spelled in large gray bold letters outlined with thick white lines. A cartoon sketch, Betty Boop style, of a girls face with fluffy black hair, long eyelashes and bright red lips sits between the words Deja and Vu. Below the sketch of the girl was a thick red rectangular bar that had the text *FASHION GIRL* written on it in white.

I needed beers.

CHAPTER 12

Two days later.

"Hello! My name is Jeff. Do you speak English?" I said.

"Yes, I speak English," said the voice on the other end of the phone.

I'd Googled "wedding photographers Salerno."

On my third try I reached Emiliano Russo.

"Excellent. I'm an author songwriter from Seattle and will be in Salerno for at least a month. I want to do a photo shoot with a model on the Amalfi coast for a music video. Can you help me?" I asked.

"Yes, I can do this," said Emiliano Russo. He spoke with a rich, artistic, Italian accent.

We had a conversation about my project and what Damin and I did with Camila and the Lambo in Houston.

I told him we took photos and video for a music video called Deja vu in Houston. The photos and video in Salerno, would be used in a music video called Love Tornado.

I told Emiliano Russo it was all inspired by my pursuit of a dream.

"This sounds like the law of attraction. I love this!" said Emiliano Russo.

"Do you have models that you work with?" I asked.

"Yes. I have models that I work with on commercial projects," he said.

We discussed the type of setting I was looking for. "On the beach, in the sand by the sea," I said.

"It is too cold now for the beaches. Last month it was hot but now the days are shorter and cooler. I know where to take you. And I have some models who would do this," he said.

"I am very busy but I could do this on September 29th. We will do it in three cities along the coast. We will start at 8:00 a.m. and finish at 8:00 p.m.," he said. "This will take one day."

"How much do you charge?" I asked.

"1600 euros," he said.

"How much for the models?" I asked.

"The price includes the model. I will email you now the photos of three models and you can choose the one you like best. I already have many ideas for this Love Tornado!" he said.

How fun is this!? I saw the photo upload on my iPhone of Model #1.

Emiliano Russo wrote below it "This model has traditional, commercial beauty and I know she would have fun with this. Her schedule is flexible and she would be available."

She had straight brown hair, brown eyes and a playful smile. She was gorgeous.

I showed the photo to Fabio (I met five people

named Fabio while in Italy) who worked at the front desk at the hostel. He was in his late twentys, had brown hair and was 5'10" tall. He was a student and was studying English and music. He was a big fan of the Smashing Pumpkins and the 90's grunge scene in Seattle. We talked for hours about bands and music videos. He asked me to look over his English papers for feedback on his language skills.

Fabio thought Model #1 was incredible. He was quite amused at the whole scene.

I uploaded photos of Model #2.

It's her! I pumped my fist in the air. *She's the one!* Her name was Valentina. She was indescribable. Pure exoticness. Long, dark curly hair, sexy body, timeless eyes, ethereal Latina beauty.

I immediately emailed Emiliano. "#2 is the one!"

"I have one more to send you," he said.

"No need to send #3, I want #2!" I said.

"Really?! You already know? Without looking at Model #3?" He was surprised I didn't want to see #3.

I knew it was Valentina. I could feel it.

"I have not spoken to Valentina yet, you understand. I hope her schedule is open for the 29th," he said. "I will call you immediately once I have talked to her."

She would be available. I knew it.

———————

The next day I met Emiliano Russo at Bar Rosa Café in Salerno to give him a deposit of 800 euros and to make plans for shooting day.

"Valentina is very excited to do Love Tornado. She asked her manager at her modeling agency about the project and he said "Yes." But she was to do it anyway," Emiliano said with a smile.

"We will meet at 8:00 in the morning in Salerno and we will shoot in the city. Then we will travel to the small town of Atrani for lunch and shoot romance there. We will finish in Ravello as the sun sets," he said.

I had a week to finalize my wardrobe for the big shoot. I had my Doppelganger suit and put together my two other outfits from the Doppelganger Men's Store to change into as we moved to the different towns. Valentina would also bring wardrobe changes.

I met Mimo. He owned a shoe repair shop next to the dry cleaners that was next door to the hostel. Mimo had lived in New Jersey for some time in the 80's and spoke fluent English. I needed all my clothes pressed and he helped me communicate with the dry cleaners. We met for espresso several times at 3:00 p.m. at a café bar across the street from his shop.

Between 1:00 p.m. and 3:00 p.m., Salerno took a siesta. Most of the stores were closed during this time. I napped too.

I spent the rest of the time walking the boardwalk by the sea and having beers at Luigi's kiosk style bar at the end of the beach.

Luigi's dad owned the kiosk, but Luigi operated it. He was in his early twenties. His friends Pasquale, Ahmad and Fabio were always hanging out there turning up the music and partying.

These kids loved it when I stopped by. They appreciated that I came to their city for my book and enjoyed the tips I left them.

"Valentina will be traveling by train from Naples and arriving at the train station at 8:00 a.m. She will be coming with her younger brother who wants to be a spectator. Elio, my assistant, and I will meet you at Pure Gelato Café next to the train station at 7:45," Emiliano said.

It was a clear sunny morning as I walked from the hostel to the train station. I wore white skinny jeans, white shoes and a black V neck tee shirt. I rolled up the bottom of my pant legs a few inches, exposing my ankles and white footie socks, like all the Italian men did.

I strolled down the streets, carrying my wardrobe changes that were on hangers, pressed and professionally wrapped in plastic.

The Pure Gelato Cafe was located at the east end of the wide Corso Vittorio shopping mall street, next to the train station.

The Pure Gelato Cafe was upscale and very busy. It was a weekday, and finely dressed business people flocked to the café bar for their espresso and pastry.

I pulled up a chair at a table on the spacious outdoor patio of the café bar. I laid my clothes over the back of a patio chair and ordered a cappuccino.

I was less than one hundred yards from the train station entrance, and I had a perfect view of the foot traffic as it arrived and flowed out into the streets of the Corso Vittorio district right in front of me.

I leaned back into my chair, crossed my right leg over my left knee, and sat in the shade under the umbrella canopy .

In Italy, espresso is served in a small ceramic cup, and saucer, along with a stainless steel spoon and small sugar packet. A shot of espresso in the morning and again after 3:00 p.m. is a ritual. I had learned this from Mimo.

I reached to the table and opened the sugar packet and gently poured it into the cappuccino. Then, I stirred it slowly, in a circular motion, with the spoon.

I put a napkin across my white skinny jeans, leaned back in my chair and basked in the most absolute fairy tale moment that I could have ever possibly imagined.

Here I was on a busy, sunny, September, weekday morning, in a city in Italy, that I didn't even know existed thirty days ago, wearing white, tight as hell Italian skinny jeans, stirring sugar into an espresso while waiting at a fancy café bar for a beautiful woman to get off a train from Naples, whom I'll meet for the first time, and go play with in one of the most romantic, captivating settings in the world.

"Ciao, Jeff!" Emiliano said happily.

"Ciao, Emiliano!" I stood and we shook hands.

"This is my assistant, Elio, he will be driving us today in my car," Emiliano said.

Elio, a college student, had short black hair, stood 5'8", was trim and spoke fluent English.

"Valentina and her brother will be arriving soon.

She texted me that her train was delayed," Emiliano said.

Emiliano and Elio put their camera gear onto the table and went inside to get espresso.

I waited on the patio, staring across the street at the train station entrance, watching the crowds of people emerge.

I saw a stunning girl. It had to be her. Her walk, her style, the way she threw her hair back smiling, was as if I was watching a scene from a romance movie.

She looked happy. She was talking to a young, dark haired, good looking lad to her left. He was carrying a heavy looking clothes bag. He looked like he could easily be her brother.

"Yes, it's her," I thought as she got closer.

A total fantasy unfolding.

"Ciao Valentina!" said Emiliano, as he returned with his espresso.

I heard her say Ciao to Emiliano. Her voice was elegant, sweet, soft, sexy.

I was stunned. She was incredible.

However, this wasn't my first rodeo. After hanging out with Camila, China, and Isabella, I would not be intimidated.

"Jeff, meet Valentina!" Emiliano said.

I was standing next to Emiliano and stepped forward to greet her.

I said "Ciao" and extended my right hand towards her. She took my hand, gently pulled me towards her, wrapped her arms around me and kissed the left side of my face.

She continued the greeting, the traditional Italian double kiss, and went to kiss my right cheek.

I was caught off guard. I leaned forward to return a kiss and bumped right into her nose as she was going to my other side!

The momentum of our noses colliding, caused my forehead to smack into hers!

She was the same height as I was, which is why we bumped noses. I had never been with a woman my height before and I wasn't expecting this ancient Roman Italian greeting. I hadn't the time to practice!

One minute I'm feeling like a king in Italy, sipping cappuccino-n-sugar in the shade, the next, I'm head-butting an Italian super model.

Valentina laughed. I could see that she was a gracious, kind, warm soul with extraordinary beauty inside and out.

I changed into my black Doppelganger suit in the café's restroom. Valentina wore a tight fitting charcoal dress, a black sweater and black boots. Her long hair cascaded down her back.

Even though it was sunny, it was cool in the morning, and the buildings kept the streets shaded.

We started our shoot on Corso Vittorio street.

Emiliano directed and took photos of Valentina and me seeing each other for the first time through the windows of coffee shops and retail stores.

We noticed one another and played cat and mouse as we bypassed each other in the narrow alleyways and magic water fountains in the old town.

Emiliano took hundreds of shots that he would process in the days following the shoot.

We left the fountains and old town Salerno, and drove down the Amalfi Coast to Atrani, which is carved right into the cliffs overlooking the Tyrrhenian Sea.

Spectacular white stucco buildings resembling ancient castles and churches, were embedded into the hills. Columns, terraces, doorways, stairways, steep trails and alleyways with stunning views waited for us at every turn, revealing new, unending secret passageways and opportunities for boy to chase girl.

Valentina wore a semi-transparent, high-slit white dress that exposed the olive skin of her left leg. She had a beaded burgundy necklace that rolled down the center of her chest. I wore my navy skinny jeans and an ocean blue cotton shirt. We were barefoot as we chased and posed with each other for photo after photo. Emiliano directed and clicked away.

Atrani is where Valentina and I meet and fall in love in Emiliano's production of Love Tornado.

We were setting up to do the scene where I first speak to Valentina. She sat on a step of a wide, white, outdoor stairway that was carved out of rock. I walked down the stairs, sat down by her and introduced myself in Italian.

At the bottom of the stairway were two restaurants with outside seating for its guests.

Some diners looked up at us as they ate.

There she was, Valentina, a gorgeous model sitting up the stairs, on a step on this ancient pathway with two cameras shooting her at the same time. Emiliano taking photos and Elio filming video.

As I stood waiting for my part, I looked at all the diners looking at us!

I felt like George Clooney, enjoying every second of the fantasy.

––––––––––––

Our last stop of the shoot was Ravello. A romantic paradise in the hills with breath taking views of the sea and surrounding town.

Valentina put her hair up and changed into a short black summer dress with gold stripes. I changed into a grey collared shirt and a checkered dinner jacket that I bought at the Doppelganger Men's Store.

Valentina and I sat at an outdoor table at a café in the gardens of Villa Cimbrone, drinking wine and smiling at each other while Emiliano coordinated with the grounds keepers where we were going to shoot next. There was a wedding party there at the same time.

Since Valentina and I didn't speak the same language, we just sat, smiled, clinked our glasses and celebrated several silent toasts.

––––––––––––

I really think she was starting to fall for me.

Especially after "The Kiss."

"This is where you kiss the girl!" shouted Emiliano.

Valentina and I were standing under an old, stone, archway that had an unbelievable view of the sea in the background. Bright pink and purple trailing flowers were blooming around the arches.

"Come to her and place your hand on her jaw and guide her chin until your lips touch!" he said from behind the lens of his camera.

But as soon as my lips came close to hers, I moved slightly past her mouth and pecked her on the cheek.

I couldn't do it!

She burst out laughing. She knew I didn't want to force a kiss on her, that I didn't want to be a creep by hiring her and then kissing her without her consent.

Or, she might have wanted me to kiss her all along and I missed it.

I know if we kissed, it would have only made it more difficult to say "goodbye" in the last scene of the day, the last scene of Love Tornado.

The sun was setting and it was getting dark.

"Follow me," said Emiliano.

Valentina and I followed him to an underground stairway that was in a tunnel beneath the gardens. Dim flood lights built into the stone tunnel walls created shadows of us as we walked down the sloping stairs.

"Jeff, you stay here and lean against the tunnel wall

with your arms crossed as you watch Valentina walk away from you," Emiliano said.

"Valentina, you walk away from Jeff down the stairs, then stop, turn back, and look at him over your shoulder," Emiliano said to her in Italian.

"This is where you must lose the girl! It's a Love Tornado!"

It was just a photo shoot, a dream, all just a dream. But my solar plexus didn't know the difference.

From a humorous greeting with a stranger at a train station, in the early morning sun in Salerno, to a gut wrenching goodbye in an ancient tunnel in the cliffs of Ravello, I could feel it all. I could feel myself falling in love, but knew I had to say goodbye.

Truly a love tornado.

Earlier in the day, Valentina and I had climbed a thirty foot rock above the sandy beach in Atrani. In her white dress, she'd sat atop the flat edge of large golden anchor that was embedded into the stone, and stared out at the sea. I stood next to her, with my hand shading my eyes, pointing to the sea, watching our ship coming in.

It felt so real.

We drove Valentina and her brother Filippo home to Naples. We arrived at 11:00 p.m.

I held her in my arms for the last time, kissed her on the cheek and whispered "Addio baby."

CHAPTER 13

In the days following the photo shoot, Emiliano finished processing hundreds of photos. He met me at the Kings Cross Irish Pub in Salerno for beers. He gave me three discs of photos.

Marco, the bartender, served us pint after pint of beers on the patio and eventually joined Emiliano and me in celebrating the shooting Love Tornado.

We left the Kings Cross pub in the late evening and walked through the quiet streets of Salerno where we had created so much.

As we approached Pure Gelato Cafe, near the train station where I had first met Valentina, I turned to thank Emiliano Russo and say goodbye.

But he was gone. Like a dream, he had vanished into thin air.

It was time to go.

I wanted more. More friends, more women, more life and more magic.

I hung around Salerno a few more days.

I had always wanted to visit Buenos Aires, Argentina. I had many discussions with other travelers who had been to Argentina, including the beautiful miss Lucia. She always had a smile on her face and had the sweetest Latin accent. Lucia was a student from Buenos Aires who was studying abroad and living in Italy. She spoke fluent English.

I became friends with Lucia, while she was working

at my favorite pizza shop in Salerno.

"You must go see Iguazu Falls!" she said.

"How do you pronounce Iguazu? I asked.

I knew how to pronounce it, I just wanted to hear her talk. My god, I'm not sure what was more intoxicating, her voice or the pizza.

I bought a one-way plane ticket from Rome to Madrid, Spain...Madrid to Rio de Janeiro, Brazil... then Rio to Buenos Aires, Argentina.

I would have an eighteen hour layover in Madrid that I was very excited about. I would be landing in Madrid at 6:00 p.m. on a Friday night. I planned to party all night then sleep on my flight to Rio the next day.

My friend Fabio who worked at the Kione hostel, helped me find a shuttle bus that traveled directly from Salerno to the airport in Rome.

I said goodbye to all my friends at the hostel, to Teresa and everyone at the In Time café bar, Luigi and friends from the kiosk bar, Mimo and Elena Veronica.

Elena was an English speaking hair stylist who I met on the way out of town. She had long red curly hair and was very friendly. As Mimo and I had our final shots of espresso together, he introduced me to Elena who was also at the café bar. Mimo told her that I had come to Salerno and was writing a book.

She was so interested, especially when she found out the book was about the Law of Attraction.

"I know the Law of Attraction is true! Please, I want

to read your book!" Elena said.

She inspired me so much.

From the first moment I got off the train in Salerno, and was guided to my hostel by Eduardo, to the last moment when I left on a shuttle bus, inspired by Elena, I was completely blessed in Italy.

I sat at the back of the shuttle bus and we began the four hour drive to the airport in Rome.

During the trip we stopped and picked up another rider. She was an attractive girl with blonde hair. She walked directly down the aisle to the long bench-style seat in the back of the bus, and sat down next to me.

What was quite unusual, was that our new passenger sat so close to me, almost on me. She leaned in and snuggled her whole body up next to mine.

It was mid-October by then. I relaxed, welcoming her presence and absorbing her energy as we drove through the lush, green, burgundy, yellow countryside of Italy.

She fell asleep with her head leaning on my shoulder.

Then I fell asleep.

————————

"What do you do besides drive all day? she asks.

"I like to write. I like to travel and write books," I say.

"Oh that sounds so fascinating!" she says. "So you are a travel writer?"

"In a way, but I mostly write about a dream that I pursue," I say.

"Wow, that is interesting," she says. "What is your dream about?"

"Ha, how much time do you have?" I joke. She was only hitchhiking a few miles.

"Are your books published? I would love to read them," she says.

"Yes, the first book is called The Secret Beast and second book, the sequel, is titled Doppelganger," I say.

My head tilted back as I slept, sitting upright on the bench seat. My mouth opened and I snored so loud that I woke myself.

Another hitchhiker dream. But this dream gave me an answer.

I was so comfortable sitting next to this girl on the shuttle bus that all my resistance had subsided, and a solution-based vibration found its way into my consciousness, via a dream.

Until that moment I hadn't had clarity on what I was going to do with all the photos and video that Damin and Emiliano had taken for me with regards to Doppelganger.

I had been thinking of "episodes" and "music videos" but after waking from the dream in the back of the shuttle bus, I decided to keep it simple and just write a "book", a sequel to the Secret Beast, called

Doppelganger.

I could use the photos throughout the book.

Simple.

The shuttle bus approached the airport. The girl was awake but was still snuggled up against me.

"What's your name?" I asked.

"Concetta," she said with a pleasant smile in return as she pulled away from my shoulder.

"My name is Jeff, nice to meet you," I said.

"Where are you going?" she asked.

"Madrid," I said.

"Have you been there before?" She asked.

"No," I said.

"Oh you will love Madrid! It is easy to take a train from the airport to city central. Go to La Latina district, it is a maze of narrow lanes filled with tapas bars and cantinas," she said.

"There is a place called La Latina in Madrid?" I said, excited. Our shuttle bus had arrived at the airport and passengers began to stand up and exit the bus.

"Thank you so much and it was very nice to meet you Concetta." I said. I smiled again. I got up and reached for my bag above me on the luggage rack.

"Oh, this is not your airport, you are going to Madrid!" she said. "There are two airports in Rome, your airport is the next stop. Good bye Jeff!"

Concetta, got off the bus, and got her bags from the luggage storage outside the bus. Then she turned and waved to me and disappeared into the crowd.

I arrived at my airport stop, and went in to the check-in counter for Iberian Airlines which was my airline to Madrid, Rio and Buenos Aires.

The man at the desk asked for my visa for Rio in Brazil. I told him I only had a passport. I knew that Brazil was the only South American country where US citizens needed a visa but was hoping I wouldn't need one for a connecting flight.

He told me I could not travel to Argentina with a connecting flight in Brazil unless I had a visa for Brazil. I said it's only an hour layover in Rio, then asked him if I could get special permission if I promised not to leave the terminal.

He said "No."

There was a woman working next to him at the Iberian counter. She overheard our discussion and started speaking in Spanish to the guy helping me.

She was a gorgeous Latina woman.

I smiled at her.

She smiled back, as she spoke to the man helping me.

Then she picked up her telephone and made a phone call.

She started speaking Spanish again.

I smiled at her again.

She smiled back as she spoke on the phone.

She finished the phone call and turned to the man helping me and continued speaking Spanish.

I smiled at her as she spoke.

She finished talking to the man helping me, then smiled at me again..

The man helping me said "It is okay for you to travel through Brazil, please don't leave the terminal in Rio."

Then, he printed my boarding passes and handed them to me.

I smiled at him and thanked him.

He smiled back.

CHAPTER 14

I arrived as planned, early in the evening at the city center of Madrid.

I ordered a small pizza, a pint of beer and sat at a table on the patio of a pizza shop, watching the people pass by.

The sun had set and the city sparkled and glowed under the lights from buildings, billboards, churches and fountains.

I was drinking a beer on a Friday night in the center of the capital city of Spain, in complete awe. The diversity of foods, peoples, clothing, languages, was so impressive.

"Do you know where La Latina district is?" I asked the server.

He didn't speak English but pointed me in the right direction.

I walked a half mile through the narrow, winding alleys and found a very cool bar district. One bar in particular caught my eye. I went in and sat at the bar. A beautiful bartender was pouring drinks. Of course.

She spoke English. Her name was Sarah and she owned the charming bar called MajareTa with her husband, Manuel. They were actors. The downstairs of the bar had a kitchen and a small stage where she and her husband, along with other local actors performed dinner theater three nights a week.

Artistic energy filled the place. Every painting, barstool, lamp, menu item, music stand, plant and dining plate had its own story of how it came to be here.

Sarah and I had a great conversation. I asked her if any bars were open all night as I had a flight the next morning and was going to pull an all-nighter.

"Most bars will be closed but if you go to the cabaret district you will find the bars that stay open the latest."

I said goodbye to Sarah and continued exploring. I crossed the street to a bar called Dejate Liar Bar before I began my search for the cabaret district.

I walked in, rolled my small suitcase under the edge of the bar, set my backpack on top of the suitcase and sat in a stool.

I looked at the bartender, then prayed they were open all night.

She was absolutely phenomenal looking and didn't speak a word of English. Another equally gorgeous woman, a friend or coworker, sat at the corner of the bar, spoke English and helped me order.

There was a fella behind the bar who also spoke English. He could tell I liked the bartender on shift. I learned her name was Lidia.

Lidia looked like a young Madonna. She had bleached blonde semi-spiked hair with dark roots and lots of tattoos and piercings. She was exotic and really fun to look at. She had her own unique beauty. I immediately fell in love with her smile, her voice and facial expressions.

I stayed and conversed at the Dejate Liar until closing. They told me how to find the cabaret district, which was only a few streets away, and then I said goodbye to my new friends.

I found a cabaret that was open. It was packed. The room was very long and traveled deep into the building but it was only about ten feet wide. It was too narrow for me to hang out with a backpack and suitcase. I stood out in the busy narrow alley and people watched as I drank a can of Mahou that I purchased from a street vendor.

Three young male travelers from Scotland chatted with me as we stood in the alley, before they noticed two female lovers mashing across the street. One of the Scots named Danny, told his friends he was going to cross the street and pick up both girls.

"No Danny, don't!" His two friends said as he started crossing the street towards the girls.

"Danny, don't interrupt them!" They pleaded. They were enjoying the show.

Danny kept walking towards the girls. As he came closer to them, he looked back at his friends, and motioned with his hand, by pointing at his target, that he was going for it.

With one last gasp of hope, his friends yelled "Danny, don't!"

I appreciated Danny's effort but he didn't have a shot. Sure enough, he interrupted the girls, upset them, and they walked away.

I wandered through the streets until the subway opened, caught a train to the airport and then caught my plane to Rio de Janeiro.

The ten hour flight from Madrid was amazing. As I was deboarding the plane, I told the beautiful flight attendant that it was the best flight I had ever been on.

Free movies, music, free wine, free beer, two meals, a red fleece blanket, a nice little white pillow and stunning women everywhere.

One ridiculously sexy passenger, struggled and struggled to stow her luggage in the upper bin in the row in front of me.

She was wearing a half tee-shirt and was exposing her midriff and much more for all who dared watch.

As I stood to help her, I heard voices say "Danny, don't!" so I sat back down.

As I strolled in my white shoes through the terminal in Rio de Janeiro, I looked for the area to wait for my connecting flight to Buenos Aires.

I saw the line forming for international arrivals, and policia checking visas.

Shit. I wasn't expecting them to be inspecting visas for connecting flights once I was inside the terminal.

"No visa?! No no, NO! said the Iberia Airlines representative, as a line began to form at customs after the plane had landed. The Iberia rep was standing in front of the line, and was checking visas.

The Iberia rep was angry and scared. He was going to have to explain my situation to the rifle slinging cops sitting in their dog pound, their office, behind one-way windows.

As I tried to explain that it was his company that

issued me the tickets in Rome, he kept shaking his head "No."

"Sit."

He pointed to the area where bad people sit and wait for execution.

This is where I met Alejandro. He was 5'8'and was dressed like I was when I arrived in Salerno...wearing cargo shorts, a t-shirt and flip-flops. He had an average build and black curly hair. He had a look on his face as if he got busted for smuggling drugs.

I sat next to Alejandro for what seemed like ten minutes without saying a word. I knew the Rio policia were watching from inside their office through the one-way windows. I tried not to smile, laugh or make any other gesture that would make it seem that I wasn't taking this situation seriously. I was actually enjoying the excitement and the degree of ridiculousness that these border cops involved themselves in over a simple visa for a connecting flight.

I had no idea what Alejandro had done.

The Iberia rep walked in and out of the cop's office several times. Each time he came out, he was shaking his head in disapproval.

Finally, the head assassin and his posse came out of their office and waved at Alejandro and me to come into their dog pound.

"Sign!" yelled the assassin as he slammed papers onto his desk.

As three other armed cops stood and watched, along with the Iberia rep, I wanted to ask "Do you mind translating what these papers say before I sign them?"

Instead, I signed them as fast as I could. So did Alejandro.

The Iberia rep motioned to us to follow him.

He walked out of the office and we followed him.

We were walking fast through the now completely empty terminal. It was midnight.

With each step, I could hear the soles of the Iberian rep's shoes clicking on the tile floor, as my feet, in soft white slipper shoes, and white footies, shuffled swiftly along after him.

I could have at least uncuffed the legs on the bottom of my fancy capris before I came here. They're going to kill me just for looking good.

I wondered where we were going. Alejandro lagged twenty yards behind.

The Iberia rep kept turning around and yelling at him in Spanish to hurry up.

I was hoping they were taking us to a room full of Latina strippers dancing on tables loaded with mountains of cocaine.

I could feel the beat of the music.

We turned a corner and all of a sudden we were entering an airplane.

It was not what I was imagining.

I saw rows and rows of human heads looking at me

as if I was a stand-up comic who had told a bad joke.

Every flight attendant and passenger on the completely full plane was staring at us.

Then I realized what was happening.

They were sending us back to Madrid!

They had a fresh staff of flight attendants. The boss lady said "Sit down, we are ready for take-off."

The boss lady was not happy as she pointed me toward the bulkhead seat. Alejandro disappeared into the rear of the plane.

I'm going to make this lady smile. The plane was slowly taxiing down the runway. She was sitting in the flight attendants station facing me at an angle.

"Do you have free wine on this flight too?!" I asked.

She smiled.

I quickly made peace with being sent back to Madrid and decided I was going to get my money's worth. I partied. I laughed hard as I watched Hangover 3, and laughed just as hard watching twenty minutes (which was all I could handle) of Vin Diesel and the Rock spit testosterone all over each other in Fast 7.

I ordered several glasses of wine, stole sandwiches from the flight attendant station and had the staff smiling and serving me free Tecate in twelve ounce cans.

When I finally passed out with my little white pillow against my cheek and my red fleece blanket covering me up to my neck, my bulkhead area looked as if I had hosted a small frat party.

When we walked off the plane, the Spain policia were waiting for us with our passports at the gate. The cops stared us up and down, then handed us the papers we had signed in Rio, along with our passports that had been taken from us.

I caught up to Alejandro. "What did you do?" I asked him as we walked through the terminal.

"My passport is broken," he said.

"What?!" I said.

"Yes," he said as he showed me the cover of his Spanish passport. It had come detached from the book of pages inside it. His passport was "broken" from all the wear and tear from commuting back and forth. He was a music DJ and performed in both Brazil and Spain.

"No way?!" I said.

"Yes. There is no missing pages, they are all together, and they said it is okay when I boarded but I need to fix it. It only takes five minutes to repair it," he said.

I saw Alejandro later at the missing luggage customer service desk and he in fact, had already fixed his passport. Two staples to attach the cover to the pages, was all it needed.

Alejandro told me of a good hostel in the city.

My desire to write Doppelganger was gaining momentum. I was thinking of writing it in Buenos Aires, but those plans had now changed.

I had arrived in Madrid from Rome on Friday night. I flew to Rio from Madrid late Saturday morning. I was in Rio de Janeiro by Saturday night, midnight, Madrid time. I was then flown back to Madrid from Rio, arriving on Sunday at noon.

I decided to stay one week in Madrid to enjoy the city and make another plan. I checked into the Motion Hostel, the one Alejandro told me about.

The Motion Hostel was near restaurants, bars and retail stores near the center of town. It had a café bar on the first floor of the six floor building. I stayed on the third floor. The building was old, and it was quicker to take the stairway than the elevator.

I wanted to find Lidia, if I could only remember where her bar was at.

It was a crisp, fall, sunny day and seeing Madrid in the daytime was almost worth the round trip.

In the city center, there was a huge open courtyard. The tall buildings that surrounded the courtyard, had giant, fifty foot billboards of fashion models and advertisements hanging down the side of them. Restaurants, bars, coffee shops and retail stores occupied the street level of these buildings.

Street musicians, artists, roller skaters, tourists, food vendors, cyclists were everywhere and from everywhere.

I opened Google maps on my phone and found the La Latina district but getting exact directions to a specific destination was impossible in the endless maze of alleys, pathways and walkways.

Not knowing Spanish or being able to remember the names of the bars didn't help either!

However, I eventually found La Latina, but nothing looked familiar. I went into a pub and had a beer. A westerner pulled up a stool next to me at the bar.

His name was James. He was a pharmacist from New York. He played guitar and travels for fun. He was going to be in Madrid for one week and then was heading to Barcelona to visit a friend.

"Having a good weekend?" James asked.

"I went to Brazil and back this weekend. Other than swollen ankles from living at 30,000 feet for 24 hours, it's been a lot of fun. You got any drugs for inflamation?" I joked. "How about you?"

"This place is incredible, I've had two dates this weekend, the women here are fantastic," he said.

"Where did you meet them?" I asked.

"Tinder," he said.

"They have Tinder here?!" I said.

"Yes. It's hot, I actually have too many matches," he said.

I told James I was searching for Lidia in La Latina.

He liked my attitude and agreed to help me find her.

Within minutes, in streets packed with what felt like hundreds of thousands of people, we came upon Lidia's coworker who spoke English and who had been sitting at the end of the bar at Dejate Liar on Friday night.

JEFFREY DULLUM

She was standing at a busy street corner and saw me at the same time I saw her. "I thought you flew away?!" She said.

She was our guide back to the Dejate Liar bar.

Lidia was working behind the bar with the same fella as before and was surprised to see me. The happy look on her face stirred a feeling inside me that I hadn't felt in a long time.

James and I had beers at the bar and conversed with Lidia using Google translate, and with help from Lidia's coworkers.

The guy behind the bar kept smiling and nodding at me, as if he knew what was happening. He was giving me "go for it pal" approval.

Then Lidia was gone.

James went downstairs to the restroom. He came back upstairs and said "Did you know there is another bar downstairs?"

We ventured back down the stairwell and saw a small group of people having drinks in the corner of the bar. I saw Lidia, sitting at a table by herself eating a meal. She was on her break.

James and I tried to converse with her a little. Then he said "Hey pal, you got this, I'm heading out."

I looked back at Lidia. What happened next, I had never experienced before.

I stood across from her as she sat at the table. I took my hands and held them gently together, in two fists,

160

and lightly pounded the center of my chest. Then I extended my arms forward, slowly and freely towards her, while opening my hands and fingers.

It was as if I was giving her all of my love, or performing on stage with Boyz II Men.

It was as if, I was trying to communicate with an exotic panther in the jungle.

She understood.

The look in her eyes reciprocated that same feeling.

We pulled out our phones and friended each other on Facebook.

She saw the photo of my Doppelganger book cover on my Facebook page and pointed to it.

She was asking me "Is this you?" as she pointed to the photo.

We were communicating.

"Yes," I said, as I nodded my head.

She smiled.

I blushed.

She went back upstairs to work.

I followed and ordered a beer.

Soon, her boyfriend arrived with an adorable black, pitbull puppy.

Damn it

CHAPTER 15

It was 6:00 a.m. Sunday morning January 15th. I was waiting for a bus at the Miami International Airport.

It took me on a thirty minute ride to South Beach. And then I went to work.

At South Beach, I checked into the Bikini Hostel.

I walked fifteen minutes to the east, found a Starbucks on the beach. I sat down basked in the warm January morning sun, sipping a Pike.

I'd left my carry-on at the hostel, and brought my backpack to the beach. Inside the backpack was a large manila envelope, addressed to me from Amazon.com.

While in Madrid, I'd received texts from both Bob Bell in Port Orchard and Matt in Tacoma asking me when I was going to return. They each had roof jobs for me.

Riding the massive momentum that I'd created during my recent travels, over the next ten weeks, I did the roofing jobs and wrote the 377 page Doppelganger book.

I wanted to do something fun to release the book. I thought of having a beautiful Latina reading Doppelganger on a beach as a marketing photo.

Initially, as I was writing Doppelganger, I had the idea to go to the city of Barranquilla, in the country of Colombia.

Barranquilla is where music star Shakira is from. I liked her music and thought she would be the perfect person to do the photo.

Most of the flights to Barranquilla had connecting flights in Miami.

I had never been to Miami and decided to go there to release the book and visit Colombia another time.

Shakira would have to wait.

I had purchased a one-way flight to Miami arriving Sunday, January 15th, earlier in December before I finished writing Doppelganger.

I had no idea if the book would be completely finished or not by the 15th, and planned to have Amazon ship the final copy to an address in Miami once I was there.

Amazon actually prints the books. If I wanted my book, I had to order directly from them.

On Thursday, January 12th, I uploaded my final manuscript into Amazon's publishing app and received the finished, physical, printed version and 1st copy of Doppelganger, Friday morning, the next day!

I brought the paperback copy to Miami.

How was I going to do this? I thought as a finished my coffee.

While at the hostel, I'd changed into a t-shirt, board shorts and flip flops. It was 8:30 a.m., the sun was warmer, but it was a bit windy on the beach.

I walked along the beach with my backpack over my

shoulder.

There were very few people at the beach, just a few passersby. By noon, the beach would be packed with people celebrating Martin Luther King weekend and the Art Deco festival.

I walked past a hotel with dozens of empty beach chairs lined up in the sand, prepared to handle the crowd that would be coming.

I saw a woman walking near one of the chairs.

She was wearing a lightweight brown spring jacket, denim jeans and sandals. Her shoulder length brown hair was blowing in the wind. She stopped and looked out at the fantastic view of the ocean. As the sun was rising in the east, it brightened the white crest of the four foot waves that were crashing the shore. She looked as if she might be a guest at the hotel.

She would definitely look good with my book in her hands.

I was standing nearby, looking in her direction. She was looking in my direction.

She was a gorgeous Latina with brown hair and big brown eyes. She looked to be in her thirties.

I had an idea.

"Hi!" I said, as I slowly approached her. I pulled the manila envelope from my backpack and held it out in front of me.

"Hi, my name is Jeff, I'm an author and I've just released my new book," I said. I pulled the book out of the envelope.

I'd hoped not to freak her out. My plan didn't work.

Before I could get any further into my sales pitch, she smiled and said "No thank you."

"Ok, thank you!" I said with a fake smile.

That was so lame, I thought. No problem, she was wearing too much clothing for the photo anyway, but it was good practice.

I walked up off the beach towards Ocean Drive, the boulevard that streams upscale restaurants, Lambos, fine hotels and tourists every day of the week.

Today, sponsor booths, art displays, food vendors, cops, bikinis and cocktails, filled Ocean Drive for the annual Art Deco festival.

It was 10:00 a.m. and the street was heating up.

Beachgoers carrying their coolers, umbrellas and chairs were marching toward the ocean.

I returned to the beach.

I walked along the shore looking for talent. I wasn't going to release my book online until I had a photo of a Latina reading Doppelganger on the beach.

I looked to my right. I was twenty feet from the ocean tide. I looked to the left. I had a view of the whole beach.

The beach sloped upward from the ocean. Anyone tanning on their belly would have their head pointing uphill towards the hotels and Ocean Drive, with their butt and feet facing me and the water.

Unrehearsed, unplanned and unprepared, I looked to the left as I walked along the beach and saw two, totally amazing asses in the sand facing me.

Yes! Just what I'm was looking for.

I didn't want to walk up behind them and creep them out, so I walked fifty yards past them and then circled back around to the other side, so I could see their faces.

Please be cute. Please be cute. Please be cute, I prayed as I walked towards the girls in bikinis.

I started my sales pitch from twenty yards away as I walked towards them. They were the only two people on that part of the beach.

"Hi! Sorry to interrupt, my name is Jeff. I'm an author from Seattle and I am releasing my new book today," I said. They looked up at me. They were both cute but the one on the left was super hot.

"I came here to get a marketing photo of a Latina reading my book on the beach. I'll pay you $50 for the picture." I continued. I was standing in front of them and leaned down to hand them my very professional author business card.

They looked at the card, looked at each other, then turned back to me and said in unison "Sure, of course."

Like magic, without my saying a word, the girl on the right got up, stood off to the side, and waved her arm towards her friend who's still lying on her belly on her beach towel. "She'll do it!" she said.

An incredible move.

I took off my backpack and grabbed my book out of it. I handed the book to the girl still lying on the beach towel, asked her to open it displaying the cover, and pretend to read it.

I backed up about five feet still crouching down, and took photos of her with my iPhone.

She puckered her lips. I was hoping that she would stop, but she didn't.

"Could you raise the book up a little?" She could still pucker, but with her face buried in the book, it wouldn't be visible.

"Yes, perfect! I want the focus to be on your beautiful eyes." I said, directing like Emiliano Russo.

"Yes. Yes. One more time….raise the book… just an inch or so…there…there…so the top of the book is the same level as your nose….got it!!" I said.

I gave them an American $50 dollar bill, grabbed the book and my backpack and sprinted up the beach to Ocean Drive.

I went back to Starbucks to text Damin in Texas.

"You are not going believe this, man, but I've been in Miami for two hours and already got the photo! Which pic do you like the best?"

After a couple texts back and forth, we chose the perfect photo.

I uploaded the photo to Facebook, along with an Amazon link, and released my book online.

Doppelganger was now officially on the market.

I was so excited. I felt so satisfied to have the Doppelganger project completed and available to share with the world.

I wandered out of Starbucks, and found an outdoor sports bar on Ocean Drive, called the Clevelander. I watched the NFL championship games, including Green Bay vs Dallas, sitting in the sun.

I smiled. I celebrated.

My bill was $130.00. All I drank was beer.

CHAPTER 16

After releasing Doppelganger I stayed in Miami for ten more days...

"Good morning," said the barista as she unlocked the entrance to the Starbucks on 8th and West.

I returned the greeting, continued to the counter and ordered a tall, drip, no room Pike, a cranberry scone and a water.

I was exhausted. It was 5:00 a.m. and I had been walking around South Beach since 2:30 a.m., waiting for a Starbucks to open so I could charge my phone.

I found an outlet in the wall located at the far end of a long, eight-foot, maple table. I sat down, parked my carry-on suitcase with wheels, and my backpack, against the wall and plugged my iPhone charger into the outlet.

Within minutes, a laptop and a stack of papers were dropped right in front of me on the table.

Out of the blue, a beautiful Latina woman in her mid-twenties pulled up a chair directly opposite me, and sat down.

There were no other customers in the coffee shop.

Wtf?, Why on earth is she sitting here when the whole store is empty?

She opened her laptop on the table and started flipping through a stack of highlighted white pages that lay to the left.

I could extend my left arm and rest the palm of my

left hand on top of her stack of papers. That's how close she was to me.

I was facing towards the inside of the store, and she was facing the windows.

She stared at the screen of her laptop. If she glanced up one inch, our eyes would lock.

I couldn't look straight ahead without staring right at her.

There was still no one else in the store!

Does she want the outlet I'm using when I was done? There were plenty of other outlets in the place. No. She must like me.

As I had walked thru town between 2:30 and 5, I had the idea to meet a woman, ask her out for dinner and take her to one of the fine restaurants on Ocean Drive.

I'd wanted to eat at one of those places, but preferred not to dine alone.

I'd needed to focus on something positive during those early morning hours. I wanted to change the crazy energy I had just experienced.

Twenty hours earlier I'd started a one-way trek to the Florida Keys from South Beach that would include four Metro buses and a Metro train ride that took me to a town called Marathon. Marathon is located midway down the Keys.

I had a friend named Johnny that I had met on MySpace ten years ago through my Count Gilbert music site. He was a fan. and had invited me to St. Petersburg, Florida, to perform, on many occasions. I never took him up on it but appreciated his invites.

He'd recently been living in Marathon.

I'd contacted Johnny on Facebook and said that I would be in South Beach to launch my new book Doppelganger.

I'd decided to take the trip from South Beach to Marathon and check it out. He lived on a ship that he was restoring. The ship was anchored four hundred yards offshore.

Johnny had invited me to stay with him on the ship. There were plenty of paint jobs if I wanted to work.

I got to Marathon at 5:30 p.m.

Johnny, was waiting for me on his bicycle.

The plan was to meet me at the bus stop then walk to his canoe that was stashed onshore. We were going to load my carry-on and backpack into the canoe and paddle to the ship.

"Dude, I was in such a hurry to get here to meet you I must have forgotten my wallet on the ship, I didn't have time to row back to get it. Do have a hundred bucks on you?" Johnny said, slapping his back pocket.

"No," I said hesitantly.

"You don't have $100 cash on you?" he said.

"No, I don't carry a lot cash on me when traveling, but I got credit cards," I said.

"Do you have a card that you can get cash back on?" he asked.

"Well yes, but..." I didn't know how to answer as I stared at a Wells Fargo ATM sign (my bank) that hung directly behind his head. "No." I said.

I didn't know what was going on. I offered to buy whatever he needed, but I didn't want to give him cash.

For some reason he needed cash.

He looked disappointed, but not upset. I followed him. I walked while pulling my carry-on, as he pedaled slowly down the side of the main road.

"I need to meet Dave up the road, then we'll go to the canoe. If you want beer, we should get it now because I don't have any onboard the ship," he said.

"No, I'm fine, unless you want some," I said.

"No, I don't drink anymore. I just smoke cocaine," he said.

"You free base cocaine? I asked.

"Well, if that's what you want to call it. I am much more creative and my third eye opens much easier with cocaine. I hope you're not afraid of rats," he said.

Rats!? How the hell am I going to get out of this one?

"Ratty lives on the ship and has never been around other people. So, I hope he'll come out and meet you," he said.

Magically, Johnny found his wallet in the basket of his bike. "Wait here," he said.

I stood outside the Hurricane Restaurant and waited. Johnny pedaled across the street to meet Dave at a strip mall parking lot.

Johnny returned in exactly three minutes.

"I got a $100 a day habit, but its way better for me than beer," he said. His whole body was tweaking like an out-of-balance washing machine.

Welcome to the Keys.

I continued walking on the side of the road, following Johnny on his bike toward the canoe. *I am not getting on a fucking ship 400 yards from shore with this freak show, and a rat?* I needed to escape.

A friend of Johnny's came up behind us.

"Hi Mary, meet Jeff. He's a friend of mine from Seattle," Johnny said.

We said hi to each other.

"Mary, and her husband Stanley, live on a ship just fifty yards from mine," said Johnny. "Is Stanley picking you up with the dinghy?" he asked Mary.

"Yep, I'm meeting him at the dock…there he is now," she said pointing to the dock.

"Will you and Stanley give Jeff a ride to my ship? I'm not sure his luggage will fit in my canoe," Johnny said.

"Sure," said Mary.

"Ok great. I'm gonna take off and go to my canoe. I'll meet you guys at my ship," said Johnny, as he pedaled away.

I had a different plan. Just as the Stanley pulled up to the dock in his dinghy, I ran away down the street with my bags.

It was dark by then. I ran into a Kmart.

"Is there a bus that can get me the hell out of here?"

"Yes! There is a bus stop at the end of the parking lot next to McDonald's. It leaves in five minutes," said the nice cashier.

I ran and caught the bus, and got back to South Beach at 2:30 a.m.

With nowhere to stay, because nothing was open including the hostel, I walked the streets until Starbucks opened at 5:00 a.m.

So here I was. And yes, to clear my head, thinking of dining with a fine woman made me feel good. And now at 5:00 a.m., this hottie sits down next to me?"

I drank my coffee. I thought that I'd say hi to her before I left.

She was very focused in her work. She wasn't wearing make-up. She had long brown curly hair that was tucked behind her ears. Wild strands from her bangs trickled down over black eyeglasses that rested on her small nose.

"Are you editing something?" I asked as I broke the ice.

"No." She smiled, lowering the screen of her laptop to look to me. "I'm studying for the Florida bar exam."

"You're lawyer?" I fell in love with her rich Latin accent.

"Yes...if I pass," she said and smiled again.

For the next 30-45 minutes we talked.

She was from Madrid.

Now, I was totally in love. She was huge into the law of attraction. I gave her my first signed copy of Doppelganger, I knew I was going to ask her to dinner.

Then she told me another story.

"I must tell you this story!" she said, as she rolled the "r" in "story."

"I told myself I never want to marry. I don't believe in it," she said.

"There is this guy who really liked me. But he's older than me and I didn't want to marry him," she continued. I interrupted her, pointed to her ringless wedding finger and said "Obviously you broke his heart, I don't see a ring."

"Listen. Listen! Listen to my law of attraction story!" she said impatiently. "We just got married 6 months ago!"

Oh, shit. I thought.

My desire to take a beautiful Latina to dinner in South Beach had just expanded.

———————————

"Where are you going?!" asked Doug.

Doug was a good friend that I had met staying at the Bikini Hostel. He was from Boston. He was a chef and had come to Miami for the winter to work.

We purchased many beers…PBR's, from the CVS pharmacy across the street, and partied on the sidewalk outside our hostel room door, or on the giant hostel patio in the center of the property.

Warm nights and flood lights found us at one of the many hostel picnic tables or outdoor pool tables with fellow travelers, Brittney, Francisco and Jacqui.

There on the patio, you could order burgers, use Wifi and hear stories from people traveling the world. When we ran out of PBR, the three cute Romanian girls who operated the hostel bar always had more.

"I'm going to Ocean Drive and find myself a dinner date," I said.

"Good luck man! By the way, you clean up well!" Doug laughed.

I was wearing my white skinny jeans, white shoes and a grey collared shirt. I had been in Miami seven days and walked the five mile boardwalk in front of the hotels every day. I was sporting a nice tan, just released my book and was feeling absolutely fantastic.

I strutted, strolled and skipped my way down the street towards Ocean Drive.

I felt like John Travolta. It was Saturday night and I had fever.

It was 5:00 p.m. People were everywhere.

Restaurants and bars are lined up one after another on Ocean Drive. Colorful awnings, patio tables, umbrellas, valet, hostesses, tourists, exotic cars, blanket the sidewalk and streets.

I'd walked up and down Ocean Drive many times in the week that I had been there. The sidewalk was always busy with the stopping and starting of tourists walking, shopping and looking to dine.

Standing in front of every restaurant was an attractive hostess selling her restaurant's daily specials. She had menus in her hand, and was ready to seat and serve.

It was difficult to walk by these girls without chatting it up with them. They were cute, and they'd walk right up to me while trying to sell food.

I was feeling so confident.

I focused as I walked down Ocean Drive, looking for any woman who looked available for dinner.

I walked past the Kantina restaurant and saw their hostess outside on the sidewalk. I had seen her earlier in the week. She was a stunning Latina with long black hair, cocoa brown skin and full black eyebrows. She was the sexiest, most spectacular girl I had seen in Miami. She wore tight white jeans, a black low cut sleeveless top and almond colored running shoes. She had a wide black watch on her left wrist and a shiny emerald green bracelet around her right wrist.

I had an idea.

I walked up to the hostess and used my new pick-up line.

"Hi, my name is Jeff. I'm an author from Seattle and came to South Beach to release my new book," I said, and I handed her my very professional author business card.

"I need a photo of me walking into a restaurant with a beautiful Latina. I will pay you $40 if you'll help me. It will only take a few minutes," I said.

"Sure!" she said with a smile.

"What's your name?" I asked.

"Maria," she said.

"Is your manager available Maria? I want to get permission so I don't get you in trouble," I said.

Within seconds the manager arrived, another gorgeous woman. I explained to the manager what I wanted to do. She said "Of course."

What happened next blew my mind.

Before my eyes, the manager turned into a film director.

"Everybody stop," she said, as she blocked the sidewalk from any foot traffic walking into the scene.

"Ok, I want you both to walk towards me toward entrance of the restaurant. I want you holding hands, hugging, laughing like you are having fun on a date," she said.

The scene was incredible. Yellow awnings hung above us, white patio tables with umbrellas and matching yellow chairs surrounded us.

The male wait staff wore white pants with yellow tee-shirts and black top hats. The female staff, including Maria, wore white pants and black tee-shirts.

Our tight white jeans matched.

Beats from the street were thumping in the background.

"One more time! Hold her hand. Then, point to the restaurant, look straight ahead and walk towards the entrance," she said.

Everyone was watching as if we were movie stars, filming a real movie!

No one noticed we were recording with an iPhone!

I gave Maria $40 dollars, a big hug, and skipped away down the street.

I didn't find a woman to dine with. Instead, I got to hold hands, hug and play with another drop-dead gorgeous Latina.

I was satisfied.

CHAPTER 17

I pull over to the side of the road to pick up a hitchhiker.

My passenger door swings open. A girl with two shopping bags jumps into the front passenger seat, then quickly fastens her seatbelt.

She's in her mid-twenties and is quite disheveled, messy hair, wrinkled clothes.

She's in a hurry. She says "Hello," as I accelerate down the road.

She says she needs a ride to an address in Bellevue. I put her destination into Google Maps on my phone that hangs from a windshield bracket in front of me.

I notice she seems disoriented, as I see the directions appear on the screen of my phone.

"Is everything all right?" I ask keeping my eyes on the road.

She doesn't smell of alcohol and doesn't appear to be under the influence of any other substance.

I stare forward at traffic, but can see her head turn and look at me.

"I used to drive," she says.

"Oh really?" I say.

"Ya, it was like a video game to me," she says.

"Wow, that's the way I feel about it too," I say.

There is dead silence as we drive onto the I-90 floating bridge that crosses Lake Washington towards Bellevue.

It is 7:00 p.m., winter time, pitch black outside and inside except for my dash lights, headlights and our illuminated phones.

I see her head turn away from me and she says "You don't have to kill anymore!"

She repeats herself, twice, in an angry, scolding voice. She is having a conversation with her imagination.

"You don't have to kill anymore!" she says again.

I agree, please don't kill anymore. I stare straight ahead at the white lines that now seem to be coming at me faster and faster.

There is complete silence again as we enter the Mercer Island tunnel.

I look back and forth from the road to her hands, holding onto the shopping bags that are between her legs. I rest my right hand on the parking brake.

Then my directions to Bellevue disappear off the screen on my phone.

The screen is blank.

I turn and look at her as she stares at her phone that's on her legs.

"My directions are gone, the screen's blank," I say, as I begin to panic.

"Ohhh," she says.

"I don't see your destination address," I say.

She looks at me, and says very slowly in an authoritative tone "The Bellevue Airport."

Great. There is no airport in Bellevue!

We are now cruising mid-span on the concrete floating bridge that is surrounded with darkness.

"Bellevue Airport huh? I have no idea how to get there now that my directions have disappeared from my phone," I say.

"Go this way," she instructs as she points, and raises her phone displaying Google Maps.

I glance at her phone and it says our arrival time would be in two and a half hours.

Bellevue is only a twenty minutes away.

The random destination address she is using is set to "walking mode" in Google Maps. Instead of a solid line, it's all dots that represent travel by foot.

"Wow, two and a half hours?" I say, looking straight forward.

I can feel her staring at me.

"Two and a half hours?" I ask again.

"Nobody has to know," she says in a slow, monotone voice, as she looks up and down at my body.

I feel like she is ready to devour a delicious meal.

We near the end of the floating bridge.

I don't feel safe. I need to get off the main road and closer to people, I want witnesses.

There is a left turn carpool lane exit at the end of the bridge. That exit connects to Bellevue Way, a local street a couple miles from the city of Bellevue.

I see a Chevron station that stands alone at the junction of the bridge off- ramp and the beginning of Bellevue Way.

She believes there is an airport in Bellevue. Trying to convince her otherwise is pointless.

I didn't want to die.

Suddenly, I have an idea.

I need to join her in her world.

I need to create an airport.

"I'm sorry, I didn't realize the airport was a two and a half hour drive. We are going to need more gas, do you mind if I stop and refuel?" I ask.

"No! Not at all!" she says with a smile.

Her mood, body language, her whole demeanor, instantly changes. She seems happy, excited.

She sits up straight in her seat and watches as I pull into the Chevron station.

There are two cars getting gas at one of the islands.

I drive around to the far side of the empty island and pull up to the pumps.

"All right, we're here! We're at the airport!" I say, like a parent adding a boost of enthusiasm to a kid arriving at the zoo.

"Thank you so much for the ride!" she says, sounding joyful.

She opens the door, hops out, grabs her bags, smiles and says "Thanks again, have a great evening!" She slams the door and walks away towards the rear of my car.

I can't see her. I immediately drive off toward the Chevron exit.

As I exit the station onto Bellevue Way, I look in my rear view mirror.

I see her.

I watch her open the rear door of a four-door Lexus Sedan and climb inside the car!

Within seconds I see a teenage boy jump out of the backseat of the Lexus. He stumbles around on the pavement in a daze looking as if he just saw a ghost.

Man, I got to help this kid.

I put my car in reverse and back up to the boy still stumbling around on the pavement.

I stop the car and just as I am about to get out, an older man jumps out of the front of the Lexus.

He too looks befuddled.

He looks like he could be the boy's dad.

I roll down my window and say "Hey bud" to the dad.

He steps over to my car.

"She's a hitchhiker, I just dropped her off. She appears to be a little out of sorts," I say.

"Thank you, I appreciate you telling me," he says sounding relieved.

I resonate with him as he scratches his head thinking of what to do next.

I figure I can save him some time.

"She thinks she is at the airport. Tell her that you are the captain and that the plane has just landed. Tell her it's time to get off the plane, and thank her for flying with you."

A hand touched my left shoulder. I awoke and jumped straight up in my seat.

"Sir, please fasten your seatbelt, the captain has announced we are about to land in Bogota," said the flight attendant.

"Another hitchhiker dream. Wow, that one was scary," I thought.

CHAPTER 18

I landed in Bogota at 11:00 p.m.

I hadn't made any reservations for a room, at a hotel or a bed at a hostel because I wasn't sure I would make all my connecting flights on my budget flight from Seattle to Bogota.

I flew Alaska Airlines from Seattle to Los Angeles, then boarded an American Airlines flight from LA to Dallas, then took a connecting American Airlines flight from Dallas to Bogota.

I planned to stay in Bogota one night and catch a flight to Cali, Colombia the next day.

I only 45 minutes to switch planes once I landed in Dallas.

My flight from LA to Dallas was delayed fifteen minutes. As I sat in LAX, I did the math.

I had 45 minutes in Dallas (all my bags were carry on) to get off, and board my flight to Bogota. There's only one flight every evening from Dallas to Bogota...which arrived in Bogota at 11:00 p.m.

If I missed the flight to Bogota, I would spend the next 24 hours in the Dallas Fort Worth airport.

45 minutes, minus 15 minutes for the delay, gave me 30 minutes. The gates closed 10 minutes before take-off.

Once I landed in Dallas, I would have 20 minutes.

This is why I didn't book a room in Bogota.

As my American Airlines flight took off from the runway in LA, the captain spoke over the intercom: "Ladies and gentlemen, we have wonderful skies ahead and it looks like we are going to make up for the slight delay, and get you to Dallas on time so you can catch all your connecting flights."

"Cool, that gets me back to having 35 minutes," I thought.

I was seated towards the front of the plane in row 13. That would help.

As we started our descent into Dallas, I told the flight attendant about my time issue.

"Sir, I will do the best I can, however, your connecting flight is an international flight and is in another terminal."

Oh, that's right. Good point, game over. I lost all hope.

"But, I will ask the captain if he can call ahead and get you an escort," she continued.

I smiled and thanked her.

I had bought the cheapest ticket on the internet, from a third party, and they are going to get me an escort?

I felt important.

The plane landed at 5:00 p.m. My connecting flight to Bogota departed at 5:40 p.m. I had 30 minutes to get to my international gate before it closed.

As the plane taxied to the terminal, I unfastened my seatbelt.

The plane pulled up to the gate and stopped. I stood up and grabbed my backpack. The flight was completely full, so my carry-on had been taken from me and checked in LA. I would catch up with it at the baggage claim in Bogota.

I hadn't heard from the flight attendant about my escort. "How rude, don't they know who I am?" I humored myself.

Because of my conversation with the flight attendant, everyone near me on the plane knew of my situation and let me squeeze by them in the aisle.

"Where is my escort that you promised? Have you forgotten that I have salsa lessons to attend?" I imagined saying as I approached the captain and the flight attendant who were standing in the front of the plane.

"Did you find an escort?" I asked the flight attendant.

"You won't need an escort sir, it seems your international connection is the gate right next to this one," she said.

"Really?" I said.

"Yes, your plane is next door," she said with a smile.

I gave the flight attendant a wink of approval as I left the plane.

Not really. Instead I happily thanked her, squealed

like a little girl, and rushed up the corridor into the terminal, took a left to my gate, flashed my passport and boarding pass at the attendant, ran down another corridor onto my international flight and sat in my seat.

It 5:05 p.m. I was 35 minutes early.

Unbelievable.

Going to Colombia was a good decision.

However, I'd be lying if I didn't say I wasn't a little nervous. There was some negative emotion brewing inside me for other reasons.

My generation had grown up with a lot of unpleasant media about chaos and upheaval in Bogota.

In my youth, I'd learned to believe that America was simply the best and safest country and everyone else just runs around, blowing shit up and killing each other.

And from my research on YouTube and learning a little history of the cartels, Escobar etc., from a guy named Jimmy that I lived with in Nashville who fled Bolivia after living in South America for 4 years, after his friend was found dead in a river, I felt a little freaked out.

Perhaps the media had some truth to it.

As I landed in Bogota, this fearful vibration became very active in my stomach.

That's probably what that scary dream meant.

I got off the plane and found my carry-on at the baggage claim.

I had one chore to do before I sat down to search online for a room using the airport Wifi.

I needed to convert some cash dollars to pesos.

I found a money exchange window near baggage claim. This was not a third party, high fee exchange, it was government run. I had to state the purpose of my visit and the length of my stay.

A very nice lady behind a protective piece of plexiglass asked when my return ticket was. I opened my confirmation email on my iPhone and slid it under the glass to her through the stainless bowl that was cut out of the counter top.

It got stuck. With me pushing and her pulling, she got it.

"Is this an iPhone 7?" she asked.

"7 Plus with a protective Otterbox," I replied.

Impressed, she smiled. We struggled to get it back under the window to me.

The struggle was fun. She was cute.

I received my pesos, then walked to a seat by the exit doors.

I found a hostel in Bogota fifteen minutes from the airport with decent reviews. I booked a room.

Just as I was finishing up, an elderly lady walked up to me. The woman had long gray hair that sprawled onto her shoulders. She wore a long dark green coat that hung to her knees. She was hunchbacked and moved slowly when she approached me. She spoke

English well enough for me to understand her.

She wanted to know if I needed a hotel room.

"No thank you, I just found a room," I said.

"Do you need a taxi ride?" she asked.

"Yes," I said, but I'm going to use Uber."

The elderly woman remained standing in front of me.

As I was trying to get my Uber app to accept my payment, a short, heavy set elderly man wearing a black sport coat, gray pants and black dress shoes, came to her side.

I tried and failed for the 3rd time to get Uber to accept my payment on my app.

"My friend drives for Uber," she said.

"Really?" I said, but how do I pay? The app isn't working…I will pay you direct," I answered my own question.

The woman nodded at her companion. I followed him out the exit doors to the parking lot.

"Hmmm, why is he not parked near the taxis at the front of the airport?" I asked myself.

I felt a vibration of suspicion and fear building momentum in my chest.

We walked for a couple minutes and arrived at his car. He opened the hatch and put my carry-on and backpack inside.

He got in the driver's side and beckoned me to sit in the front passenger seat. I got in.

Something did not feel right.

Where was this guy's phone and Uber app? Certainly he must have an Uber app if he drives for Uber.

"Where is your Uber app?" I said as I pointed to the Uber app on my phone. He didn't seem to understand.

I repeated my actions.

Finally he pulled out his phone and pointed to the Uber app on the screen.

It was not the drivers app. It was the rider app.

My fears and suspicion increased, then a manifestation ensued. I took action.

"Open!" I said, as I got out of his car. "Open the hatch, I want my luggage!"

He got out of the driver's seat and opened the hatch. I grabbed my carry-on and backpack and hurried away.

I walked back to the row of taxis in the arrivals area.

Certainly, I can trust a taxi.

I showed a taxi driver the address to the hostel and got in the front passenger seat.

The taxi drove away from the airport and onto an empty four-lane road. He was driving really fast, as was my heart.

It was completely black outside with no street lights, and no other vehicles on the road.

I was getting more scared by the minute.

We passed a Sheraton Hotel and a part of town that looked habitable.

We continued to drive on, into the darkness.

I began to see building after building that looked at least forty years old. Each one had black iron security gates. All the doors, and windows were behind iron bars.

Nothing looked safe…vandalism, graffiti, it looked like a war zone.

We kept driving. More blackness.

The faster my heart raced, the faster the taxi driver drove.

I was experiencing and perceiving exactly what I feared.

"Negative momentum is like jumping out of an airplane without a parachute. Don't worry, it will all be over soon." The Abraham-Hicks quote came to mind.

We came to another scary looking part of town and the taxi driver slowed down. He turned off the main road, and it appeared as if he was looking for the address of the hostel.

"Where are you taking me?!" I asked.

"Relajarse, relajarse," the driver said.

"No, no, no! Go! Turn!...fucking turn around...turn the fuck around NOW!" I demanded, as I raised my right hand and swirled it round and round in the air.

"Relajarse! Relajarse!" he said over and over again.

What was he saying?

"Back! Go back...Sheraton! Go to Sheraton now!" I continued.

The driver reached down and started to pull an object out from under his seat.

I raised my left hand and was ready to pile drive him into the driver's side window. I though he was pulling out a gun.

Instead of a gun, he pulled out a large flashlight and started shining it on the front of the buildings. He was looking for the address!

Damn, I thought he was pulling out a gun!

I said "Me relax?" as I extended my arms, opened my hands and lowered them slowly to my lap "Me? Relajarse?"

He smiled and nodded as if he understood and said "Yes."

I pointed to him and said "You," then pointed to myself and said "No kill me?" as I took my hand, finger extended and brought it across my throat.

He laughed and shook his head.

This was very, very comforting.

Even so, I knew this part of town was not where I was going to be sleeping.

The street was deserted without a single light on. There was no way a hostel was going to be located in this part of town.

"Airport! Go back to airport!" I said to him.

He looked disappointed.

I wanted to go to the airport and fly back to Seattle.

Was learning salsa worth that kind of fear? I had never been so afraid in my entire life.

He motioned to me that he wanted to circle back through the neighborhood and try one more time.

He turned left down an alley. I saw a light from a bare lightbulb on the outside of one of the buildings.

"Over there, a light," I said.

He stopped the car.

I looked back and saw the word "Republica" on a sign below the light.

"That's it! Back up!"

The driver put the vehicle in reverse, and as we backed up, I saw a young man open a large, black iron gate in front of the building and was motioning to us.

This was Ricardo, the hostel clerk.

He had received the booking confirmation online and was waiting for me.

I paid the taxi driver and he drove away.

Ricardo gave me a warm welcome in perfect English.

I had created my own fear because my pre-conceived beliefs of a violent city. The darkness, iron gates, history of the country and warnings from friends had a strong influence on my perception.

The Law of Attraction is exact and momentum ensued until it manifested first in my dreams, then my reality.

The good news is that in doing so, I was simultaneously creating a vibrational version of the exact opposite.

In perfect balance, I was creating the possibility of love, security and joy.

There are two ends to every stick of "wanted" and "unwanted."

My fear would serve me in search for love.

"How can you know what you want until you know what you don't want?" –Abraham-Hicks.

If I could achieve this positive emotional state by focusing on the positive side of the stick, I could experience more love, than I could ever imagine.

CHAPTER 19

As I returned to the hostess station after my closing dinner shift to grab my backpack with my t-shirt, board shorts and flip flops stuffed inside, I heard a voice behind me say "Jeff, give Chris a hand before you go okay?"

It was the general manager Art, asking me to help set up the dining room for dancing.

Changing out of my sweaty server uniform, black pants, black polo and black shoes and going downstairs to have beers with my friends in Mello's bar, was going to have to wait.

It was Friday night at the Paradise Grill in Kaanapali, Maui. Every Friday night when the restaurant stopped serving dinner at 10:00 p.m., it hosted dancing until 2:00 a.m.

"Thanks for helping, Heffe," said the young Polynesian busser named Chris who always called me Heffe.

As we carried the tables and chairs from the restaurant and stacked them outside on the lanai, a crowd began to form outside the main entrance.

Once we cleared the wooden dining floor, we marked off the dance floor with masking tape. I held one end of the 3 inch roll of tape as Chris hurried across the floor with the other. We stuck 20-foot long pieces of tape to the floor and formed a square that represented the dance floor.

It was Salsa night.

Sharply dressed, enthusiastic dancers began to filter

into the room filling up the booths that lined the walls of the restaurant.

The DJ had just finished setting up his gear and the thumping Latin music began blasting through the speakers.

I wanted a Margarita.

Who are these beautiful people? I stood, watching the dancing begin.

I had never seen these people in our restaurant or anywhere else on the island except on Friday nights. I certainly would have noticed because the women were incredibly sexy, gorgeous, and dressed to kill.

The men wore cologne, and were confident, and proudly dressed. They were serious dancers.

As I stood there, a smelly server, I was jealous, and realized I didn't have shot of hooking up with any of these ladies.

After watching a few minutes of the action from the sidelines, and as the women began to turn me on, I went downstairs and ordered a Bud Light.

I couldn't handle anymore.

I wanted what they had. They were having an absolute blast.

If I wanted to be with a Latina, I needed to learn how to Salsa dance. Learning a little Spanish would also help.

"One, two, three, pause, 5,6,7 pause...One, two, three, pause, 5,6,7 pause...back two, three, pause, back 6,7 and line two, three pause and line 6,7 good!" said Angela, my salsa instructor.

Four years later I found myself in the city of Cali, Colombia in South America, a place some call the "salsa capital of the world," learning the fundamentals of this art form from a world class professional.

"I'm a little hung over," I said as we began our 2 hour daily session. "Four of us went out last night to La Topa Tolondra and I tried out the new skills you're are teaching me."

"You did?!" Angela said.

"Ya, but I sucked! Do you have any idea what it feels like to grab the hands of girls sitting at tables, escorting them to the dance floor, and then watching the disappointment on their faces when they learn that I can't dance, or speak Spanish?!" I said.

She laughed. She understood.

"I couldn't even explain to them that I'm just a beginner!" I continued.

"No, no, no! You have...umm...how do you say? reedem?" she said.

"Rhythm?" I said.

"Yes, you have reedem! Not many people have this, they just off somewhere else not listening to the beat," she said as she walked across the room to turn on the music again.

As I was about to say "thank you," she turned,

smiled, shook those hips at me sexily as she grabbed
my hands and said "5,6,7 and one..."

I stayed the night at the hostel in Bogota then caught
a flight to Cali the next morning.

I grabbed a taxi, then the taxi driver and I made the
forty-five minute trip from the airport to the Casa
Miraflores hostel. I pulled out my phone to follow our
trip on Google Maps. The driver didn't speak English
but motioned for me to put it out of sight.

In this area, thieves on motorcycles reach into
vehicles with the windows down and steal phones. I
learned quickly that my iPhone was worth a lot of
money in this part of the world.

I arrived at the hostel at 12:00 noon.

I was amazed at how beautiful the three-story hostel
was. It had waterfalls, plants, flowers, Zen paintings,
couches and pillows. Wide stairways made of iron
connected the floors. A monster wooden dining table
and chairs sat in the dining room. A tall round wooden
bistro table and chairs, and a computer desk were in the
lobby adjacent to the dining room.

It had a salsa dance studio, a yoga studio, a small
library, and multiple areas for quite meditation.

Large, modern kitchens with granite counter-tops
and stainless steel appliances were located on all three
floors.

As I checked in, I noticed a sign that said "Salsa
classes daily at Casa Miraflores!"

"Can I get private salsa lessons?" I asked.

"Yes." said the friendly English-speaking girl working the counter. I later learned her name was Paula.

"Can I get classes every day for two weeks?" I asked.

"Yes, each class is two hours long," she said. "I will sign you up for today at 2:00 pm!"

Wow, that was easy.

But I had another very important question to ask her.

"I hope you don't mind me asking you, but, are the salsa instructors guys or girls?" I said.

"Girls, and they're hot," said a voice from behind me.

I turned around and saw a man in his mid-thirties sitting at the circular wood bistro table.

We introduced ourselves. He beckoned me to sit with him. He was the owner of the hostel and had been in Colombia for seven years. He purchased the building five years earlier and had completely remodeled it.

His name was Nate. He was a contractor from Bellingham, WA. near Seattle.

As we talked, a girl walked into the room and asked Nate a question in Spanish. He answered in Spanish, and she walked away. As we continued our conversation, he seemed oblivious to what I had just witnessed.

The girl who had spoken to Nate was so intoxicatingly beautiful, that words could not even begin to describe her!

But I'll try.

She was 5' 3" and had long straight jet black hair that flowed past her waist. She had mysterious dark eyes and arched black eyebrows. She was wearing tight black spandex shorts and a tight pale pink cropped tank top that showed off her milk chocolate skin. Her soft rich Spanish accent arousing. Her body...

She was freaking ridiculous.

She was my dance teacher.

JEFFREY DULLUM

CHAPTER 20

I was frustrated.

It was my fourth daily two-hour salsa lesson in as many days and even though I had learned more salsa in those four days than I could possibly expect, I felt my brain and footwork weren't harmonizing.

Angela walked over to the sound system and turned off the music.

She returned to me, grabbed my hands and stood toe to toe facing me in "beginning position."

While holding my hands, with the top of her head almost bumping my nose, she looked up into my eyes and began to speak slowly and calmly as if the patience of the universe was flowing directly through her.

"Try again slowly, without music. You must have confidence. You must let the energy go to you and no thinking, relax, you must be confident or you cannot do salsa."

My frustration disappeared as I stared into her eyes and appreciated the fact that I had just popped an Altoids peppermint breath mint.

"Confidence," I said, as I exhaled into her face.

"I am confident, that I will be confident, as soon as I learn the steps," I said.

"It's no problem, you are doing good," she said.

We finished the lesson. Then I walked down the hallway to my room, changed out of my sweat soaked tee shirt, grabbed my phone, and water bottle and ran back to the studio where she was packing to leave.

I interrupted her as she reached for her motorcycle helmet.

"Do you have a minute?" I said.

"Of course," she responded.

I opened the calendar on my iPhone.

I pointed to the date May 22 and said "I go back to the United States one week from Monday. I want to be sure you can give me two hours of salsa every day until I leave. I want to learn as much as I can. I came to Cali only for salsa because it is inspiration for a story in a book that I am writing."

"Book?" she said, as her eyes widened.

"Yes, I travel to places and write for my book," I said.

"Am I in your book?" she asked curiously.

"Well, that was going to be my next question, is it okay if I write about our lessons and use your name?" I asked.

"Yes, it would be my pleasure," she said.

"Good, let me show you something," I said.

I opened up Amazon.com on my phone and showed her The Secret Beast and Doppelganger titles that I had listed for sale.

"These are two books that I sell on Amazon and now

I am writing the next book called Bodhi," I said.

"Amazon? what is Amazon?" she asked.

"You have not heard of Amazon.com?" I asked.

"No," she said, "I would like to read your book, I have read only books for study."

The next morning I ate breakfast at The Paola restaurant, a street cafe next door to Casa Miraflores.

When I returned to the hostel, there were two notifications on my iPhone from WhatsApp, the global Wifi communication service.

One notification said that I had missed a call from Angela. The other was a text message from her, asking to move our Saturday afternoon lesson from noon to 1:00 p.m.

Angela had asked to exchange phone numbers after our first lesson.

Her English writing skills were very good.

When we finished our 1:00 p.m. session, and were arranging a time for Sunday's lesson, I noticed her texting on her phone.

"Tell me, I noticed you speak and write English very well. What skills are you the best at, reading, writing or speech?"

"Reading and writing, my speech not as good," she said.

"Wow, I'm impressed, how did you learn? From school in Cali?" I asked.

"Mostly in Spain when I lived there seven years, then three years now in Cali," she said.

"You spent seven years in Spain? What did you do there?"

"I train for salsa dance, I was on a team, there were free English classes that I take," she said.

"Really?! Seven years in Spain, training for salsa? All by yourself or with your family?" I asked.

"Me and my son."

"What did you say? I asked.

"Me and my son lived in Spain."

"You have a son?" I said.

"Yes, my son is 16 years old," she answered.

A rush of energy blasted through my solar plexus knocking the wind out of me. My torso collapsed causing my head to fall towards the floor.

My hands caught my fall. I was down on my haunches and my hands gripped my knees.

Bent over, out of air, I felt like I had just sprinted up a steep street in San Antonio, the neighborhood behind the hostel. I looked up at her and said "You have a 16 year old son?"

"Yes," she smiled proudly, "I am a single mom."

"Wow, sorry, I'm completely shocked. My brain just exploded."

"It's no problem," she smiled again.

"Again, I apologize. I didn't think you were older than 23. Especially when you said you're taking a chemistry class at the local college, I thought you were younger. I thought, well, never mind. I, of course, think it's wonderful that you are a mother," I said, as I stood up straight. "Do you realize that you look like you are 23?"

"Yes, I know this," she smiled.

"It all makes sense to me now, because when you talk, and teach, you appear to have more wisdom and discipline than a 23-year old," I said.

We agreed on a 4 o'clock lesson the next day, Sunday.

Still in shock, I showered, then went to the front patio of the hostel and sat in the sofa chair with my bottle of water.

I saw Angela again as she was on her way out to her motorcycle.

"Angela, can I speak to you?" I said.

She came and sat down next me.

"How about no lesson for tomorrow, but I will pay you anyhow. It's Mother's Day."

"Thank you Jeff." She rubbed my right thigh affectionately, stood up, put on her helmet and walked to the exit gate."

"Be careful on that bike!" I called out.

"Yes, it's no problem, goodbye Jeff!" she said as she rode off down the street.

It's her, I know it. She's the woman I have been waiting for.

The woman in my dream.

I could feel it.

I knew the woman in my dream was getting closer and closer.

My five and a half year journey to meet her, is manifesting, if not, "no problem," as she says. It's a win-win. Either it's her, or one hell of an experience to feel the possibility of it being her, shooting through my body.

The rush of energy was so intense, rich and satisfying. Years of resistant energy, the struggle, was dissipating from the cells of my body.

I couldn't stand up from the sofa for an hour.

I opened my WhatsApp chat thread with Angela and reread our conversations. I noticed the happy emojis in her messages.

"What should I do next?" I thought.

Be confident. This is the guidance that came to me earlier, directly through her.

This is when the universe stepped in. I accidentally touched the WhatsApp missed call notification, and called her number.

I quickly tapped it off with my thumb.

Ten minutes later she texted me, "Did you call me?"

Oh shit, now what?

It took about fifteen minutes to sort my thoughts, then I texted her telling her that I wanted to talk her when she had the time.

Forty-five minutes later she texted me "Oh, I was just near to the hostel teaching a lesson but now I am home on the other side of town thirty minutes from you." She had added a sad emoji.

Another text immediately followed, "I bought dinner...papaya and mango! You must taste it!" Followed by happy emojis.

"I would love that," I texted.

Immediately she responded with her address.

Boom!

"I will take a taxi and see you in one hour," I texted.

"Be careful." Happy emojis responded.

After a thirty-minute Spanish lesson from the taxi driver, on the way to Angela's, learning how to say "Bonita chicka," I arrived at her place.

"Well, here is my chance to be confident." I thought.

I sat on her couch in the small bare apartment.

She sat facing me on the couch with her legs crossed in meditation style. "Tell me!" she said.

"Where's my dinner?!" I asked.

"Oops! I ate it all!" She laughed, then stared into my eyes, as if she was waiting for me to start the dance by taking the first step.

For the next hour I explained my dream and my inspiration for being in Colombia.

I told her I had created a dream nine years ago in Gig Harbor WA. I showed her photos of the beautiful town. I told her three and a half years into creating my dream, I had split with the girl I was in love with, and had fled to cities around the country and around the world, chasing my dream and searching for the Latina to replace her.

I spoke of The Secret Beast, where I'd written about when and why I created my dream.

I spoke of Doppelganger where I'd created events with two of the most beautiful Latina girls in the world in an effort to know what it felt like to stand in the presence of such beauty.

I spoke of Lamborghini rentals and castle chasing, all to experience the feeling of satisfaction in my solar plexus.

I told her that I believed once I knew those feelings that satisfy, that I could duplicate them over and over in my thoughts, emotions and body. The Law of Attraction would duplicate those feelings, and would bring me more and more such thoughts and experiences that satisfy!

I explained that with consistency, focus and the deliberate purging of doubt and resistant thought from

my life, momentum would be attained, and Like
energies or vibrations would manifest into the see it,
hear it, smell it, taste it, touch it, reality of my physical
world.

I told her that the fact that I was having this
conversation with her, was evidence of that power
manifesting.

She understood every word.

With confidence, I looked into her eyes and said
"You are the woman in my dream. I know it."

For the first time, she looked confused and said "Are
you talking real or about your book?"

"Both," I said. "You and me together for real, which
is also, in the book. Yes. What I'm saying is that, I
really, really like you, a lot, and let's just see how far
this goes and how much fun we can have, for real."

"Yes, no problem. That is good to me," she said
smiling.

"Then I should probably take you on a date for
dinner, tomorrow night, on Mother's Day," I said.

"Yes!" she said.

Truly, I was in heaven.

JEFFREY DULLUM

CHAPTER 21

It was Mother's Day, and I had a dinner date with a gorgeous Latina, for real.

We kept our plans private from the others at the hostel.

At 5:00 p.m. I walked a few blocks from the hostel, and met Angela.

She pulled up to the street corner on her motorbike. I jumped in a taxi and she gave the taxi driver directions to Cantina La 15.

I met her in the Cantina La 15 parking lot where she parked her bike.

We entered the Cantina and the hostess walked us to a table in the front corner of the elegant restaurant. The brick building had hardwood floors, high ceilings and was quite spacious. Silver chandeliers glittered as they hung from large wooden beams in the ceiling.

Tall windows facing the street were behind us as we sat facing the bar and other diners.

The enticing menu was filled with steak and fish entrees.

"How you say…squish?" Angela asked, as she glanced at me, then back to our server as she was ordering her appetizer.

"Squish? Do you mean squid?" I asked.

"Yes!" she said.

I had only known this woman for one week and in

that "squish" moment, I'm not sure I ever enjoyed a laugh as much as the one we had together.

Dinner was magical. The South American ambience and cuisine, the woman's voice, her beauty, her style. It was pure nirvana.

Outside, I gave Angela a hug goodbye, then got into a taxi. She pulled up to the driver's window of the taxi on her motorbike, revved the engine, and gave the driver instructions to take me back to Casa Miraflores. Then she raced off down the busy street. She was such a badass!

———————

I met Angela at the hostel dance studio the following day for my two-hour lesson. The studio was downstairs in an open area near the stairs, pond and waterfall.

The hostel was quiet. There were no other travelers or staff around.

As we were beginning our lesson, I pulled Angela into the corner, where no one could witness, hugged her, then whispered "Thank you again for having dinner with me."

We finished the lesson, and she left. Later that day I received a text from her "Thank you for the hug." Five smiling emojis with heart eyes followed.

"I want to take you to dinner again," I texted.

I only had one week left in Cali.

We arranged to have dinner the following night at 7:00 p.m.

"Bring a swimsuit and a towel!" she texted.

We took a taxi up into the hills of San Antonio to a restaurant that overlooked the city. The property had a large outdoor swimming pool that extended outwards towards the cliff below the restaurant.

The view of the pool and palm trees was incredible. It was dark and the city lights sparkled in the valley below.

It was odd, we were the only people dining at the restaurant.

We sat at our table which was facing a wall of windows. We could see the pool and the city below us.

Bamboo, palm tree leaves, candles, paintings, vintage lamps, decorated the dining room. There were music videos, playing without sound, projected onto a wall.

She ordered Mojarra fish and I ordered Carne Asada.

We were served a bottle of red wine.

I wanted to know more about her.

As we sat at our table, she pointed the screen on her phone "These man cannot walk, or stand, he what's the word?...he hanth han handth..." "Handicapped," I said.

"Yes, he handicapped but now he stands and taps his feet to the music," she said, as the video played.

"And this is you?!" I confirmed, as I pointed to a female with long jet black hair that was standing next to a man dressed in white, who was coaching a boy who was moving his legs and feet back and forth with the aid of a walker.

"Yes, and these man is the doctor. He is so wonderful," she said.

I looked at the video on her phone as she explained that she was a volunteer at a local physical therapy clinic. The doctor uses music and dance therapy to help rehabilitate his patients.

At the clinic, Angela taught the patients how to move a toe or foot, to get energy to begin flowing through their bodies. In time, some could stand, with aid from a walker, and even move their feet to the salsa music that she loved.

My eyes became wet.

Volunteering was in addition to the hours that Angela spent giving private salsa lessons plus then training and performing with one of her several dance teams four to five hours every night.

She showed me videos of her shows. She was free falling vertically from the tops of shoulders, being swooped horizontally across the floor into a complex dance move, dressed in exotic costumes, Cirque du Soleil style. She danced in a group to dances that looked like Michael Jackson's Thriller on steroids.

This girl can dance, all she does is dance.

She's a teacher, a therapist, a coach, a choreographer, a teammate, an artist, a model, an athlete, and a mom-all packaged into one magnificent human dancing female body.

The energy that creates worlds, flows through her easily and continuously.

And I got to witness and participate in the exploration of her world.

We finished dinner and found the stairs that led down to the pool.

"Did you know this dance hall was here?!" I said.

"NoOOoo!" she said with an extended "oh" that rose, then fell.

We walked into the completely empty discotheque and sat at a table. The room was huge with a white tile floor, white barstools, and white tables and chairs spread around the outside of the dance floor.

Pink floodlights and loud pulsing Latin beats created a surreal vibe.

No one was there but me, her, the DJ and a bartender who came to take our order.

We had the whole place to ourselves.

We ordered a pitcher of beer.

She was wearing a little white dress with a bikini underneath. I was wearing navy skinny jeans, a short sleeved button-down shirt with blue and white stripes and white shoes.

We danced, drank beer, danced and drank beer.

Then I kissed her. Then again. And again.

"Let's go out to the pool," I said.

There was no one at the pool.

Angela removed her dress. I had a towel and board shorts in my backpack. I changed behind the pool house.

She looked unbelievable in her lime green thong bikini.

We never made it into the water.

Down to the fully reclined beach chair we went. She lay on her back as I began to massage her thighs, kissing her.

I moved my open hand down to her inner thighs then traveled up, down and around her legs, from her toes to her pelvis.

I gracefully circled my right hand and fingertips from inside her legs, through her groin area to the top her pelvis. I closed my hand as I slowly moved my fist, with gentle pressure, up her belly, between her breasts and then opened my hand again at her neckline.

Then, like swimming laps in a pool, I touched the bottom of her chin, reversed direction, and slowly moved my open hand back down between her breasts, across her tight belly and parked it on her pelvis.

The thong bikini was coming off.

At that moment, a staff person came around the corner and started lecturing us in Spanish!

I had no idea what he was saying, but his timing was terrible.

Angela jumped up and put on her dress. I hurried and changed back into my clothes as we giggled and smiled.

We left the resort and took a taxi to the upscale Torre de Cali Plaza Hotel. It was a tower in the city.

We made love.

The view of the city from our room was breathtaking. I stood by the windows in a state of complete ecstasy. I was calm.

I felt her naked body come up and hug me from behind. I felt her lips kiss my shoulder blades. I turned and held her in my arms as we stood and stared at the city.

I felt like a proud Lion King. I felt worthy, fulfilled.

I had dreamed of being with a beautiful Latina. Never did I imagine, she would be a woman like Angela.

CHAPTER 22

We fell in love.

I continued to take my two-hour, daily salsa classes.

That Saturday night we met at the Marriot bar, checked-in, and ordered room service. We never left the room. Sunday morning we had a luxury couples massage session, stretched in the sauna and dined at the hotel's five-star brunch.

I had one more night in Cali.

When weren't together, we were messaging each other. Lovers in love, doing what lovers do. We were having so much fun.

"What happens when I leave on Monday, are you my girl?" I texted.

"Of course, we are a couple. But I do not have a ring!" she texted, followed it with laughing and heart emojis.

————————

I took a taxi to the upscale Chipichape Mall.

I found a fine jewelry store. The manager who waited on me spoke English. I told him my story and that I wanted to buy a promise ring.

He hooked me up.

————————

Anglea and I booked a room at Parque La Perojosa for our last night.

It was a small resort located at the top of a mountain that overlooked the city of Cali.

The only way to get to the resort was with a four-wheel drive vehicle. The resort provided transportation, and a Jeep picked us up in Cali and drove us the forty minutes up the mountain.

The Parque resort was a spotlessly clean, simple, rustic, open air lodge with eight rooms, each with private bathrooms. The host provided a home-cooked meal and breakfast in the resort dining room.

It was a perfect hangout. We watched the sunset over the city of Cali, ate the delicious, home-cooked food, drank the beer, shared shots and watched the camp fire in the yard try to burn in the random thunder showers. I held her close as we listened to the rain beat down on the metal roof panels above us.

It was the most romantic place I had ever experienced.

The power went out during the night. We lay together by each other's side in our bamboo framed bed, by candlelight.

The next morning, after breakfast two tour guides took us repelling down waterfalls. We were in an exotic jungle, playing in the mountain water.

Afterward, Angela smiled, kissed me and said "I am so proud of us! We are professionals now!"

It was time to go.

We went back to the room, packed our belongings, and waited there for the Jeep to arrive to take us back down the mountain. Then it would be time to say goodbye to Angela, and leave to the airport.

I asked her to sit down on the bed.

I handed her a small gold gift box. The ring was inside.

"This is for you, a promise of our future," I said.

She smiled and opened the box.

"I love this! It's beautiful, thank you!" she said.

As she leaned over and kissed me on the lips, there was a knock on the door.

We were told the Jeep had arrived to take us back down the mountain.

Down the mountain we went. Parts of the winding dirt road had been washed out by the rain. Deep trenches made it a dangerous journey, even in a Jeep.

I held Angela's hand. She had put on the ring.

She looked sad. I thought it was because I was leaving.

The Jeep was picking up speed.

"I will return, I promise you," I said.

She looked into my eyes. Her face looked as if she had bad news to tell me.

"The ring does not fit, it's too big," she said.

She held up her hand and showed me the ring that fit loosely on her finger.

"That's okay...we can get it resized," I said.

"You don't understand, the ring is too big," she continued.

Just as we were turning the last corner at the bottom of the mountain road, a dirt bike zoomed around it going up the mountain. The motorbike was heading straight for the front of the Jeep.

The adrenaline-jacked rider on the dirt bike swerved hard left and missed the right front fender of the Jeep as our driver threw the steering wheel to the left.

The rider, completely unphased by his near death experience, saddled the bike quickly back and forth between his legs as he retained control in the dirt S curve at 50 mph, then gunned it harder, faster and flew past us up the mountain road.

"The ring is too big," she repeated. "The meaning is, I am not the one of your dreams." She said with heavy eyes, slowly lowering her head.

"What? I can't hear you?" I said.

Policía on dirt bikes, full throttle, flying by us up the mountain pursued the outlaw biker with a vengeance. I couldn't hear a thing.

"I am not the one," she said again.

"No! you are!" I said.

At least ten cops on bikes with sirens blaring, and blue lights flashing from the handle bars, dressed in military green uniforms, were on the rampage to catch this guy.

Our Jeep driver accelerated as he swerved back and forth to avoid the oncoming motorbikes, as they screamed past us. The speed, the sound, the scene, the rush of energy, was off the charts.

How far can the gangster go before he runs out of mountain road!

I looked down at Angela's ring finger, then looked up just as a cop on a bike was heading straight for our Jeep!

"WATCH OUT!!!"

The screen went blank. There was perfect silence.

––––––––––––

"I love you," says a soft voice coming from a dark corner.

"I. Love. You." she says again.

A dim light appears on her face. She is beautiful.

It is her.

––––––––––––

I jumped up off my mattress and went to get a glass of water.

I picked up my phone. It was 2:30 a.m., and read the text that had woken me with a bell tone.

"Hey! great to hear from you! I just got off work. I am at the Tin Hat bar in Ballard. I work tomorrow, come by and say hi."

It was from Josefina.

The next day I googled "Tin Hat", got the address in Ballard, then drove to the neighborhood in northwest Seattle.

———————————

I had met Josefina in Tacoma, six years earlier. She was a bartender at Medi's. I had just split with my wife, Alaska, who was seeing a cop.

This is when I edited my wife out of my original dream and created my desire for the Latina beauty.

Josefina was breathtakingly beautiful, had long black hair, brown eyes and a wonderful warm smile. She was intelligent, kind and had the gift of making anyone in her presence, feel good. I had met her in my darkest hour after losing my brother and wife. Hanging out and talking with her at Medi's bar was life-giving.

During my short stay in Tacoma, I hosted a concert event at Medi's. The event was a fundraiser for my niece who had breast cancer.

Alaska and I had a business together and remained friends. Alaska attended the show and sat at a table directly in front of the stage with two of her girlfriends.

Josefina was their server.

I couldn't have imagined a better set-up as I sang my song Short Stick. It's a humorous song about me picking the short stick in our broken relationship.

After the show, I thanked Alaska for coming, and then whispered in her ear "Do you know the bartender that served your table? One day, I will be with her."

"She's way too young." Alaska warned.

"You were younger when we married, it's all perception," I said.

The inspiration from that experience was incredibly motivating. I knew that I would have to transform into my "best self" to ever be with a woman like Josefina.

As I traveled in the years that followed the night at Medi's, I searched for a female companion, lover, friend that could match the positive energy and spirit that I felt from Josefina.

When I visualized the woman in my dreams, she was Latina, with long dark hair for sure, but her face was never clear.

I would text Josefina from time to time when I returned to the Seattle/Tacoma area. If she was bartending, I would visit her.

———————

On 65th St. and 5th Ave., I saw a large sign on an older building that had the Tin Man from Wizard of Oz, painted on it in black and white.

It was a cartoon style image of the Tin Man smiling and holding a full pitcher of beer in his left hand.

I parked my car.

A sign on the door read "Open daily at 4:00 p.m."

It was 4:05.

I opened the door and entered the Tin Hat.

I walked through the dimly lit dining room and sat at the bar. No one was there.

I looked around and saw dark wooden tables and chairs throughout the empty dive bar. There were two pinball tables tucked away near the restrooms in the back. Concert posters, magazine covers and game souvenir tickets, blanketed the ceilings.

A vintage Archie Bunker grandson doll, in the original box, rested next to a plastic Gene Simmons model, a box of lawn jarts, playing cards, knick-knacks, old VHS movies and other collectibles on a shelf behind the bar.

There was an old tube TV hooked up to the wall at ceiling level behind the bar that was playing a VHS of Beetlejuice. The screen was fuzzy, the volume low.

There was an entrance into a small kitchen at the end of the bar. A chalkboard with the daily specials listed on it, hung next to the doorway.

A woman walked from the kitchen into the bar.

It was Josefina.

"Hey there!" she said.

"How are you doing?" I replied.

She was absolutely stunning.

"What are you drinking?" she said.

"Bodhi, please."

She poured my beer then said "Hold on, I just have a couple more opening chores to do."

I looked around as I sipped my beer. A rush of deja vu came over me, flooding my senses with feelings of returning home, as if in a dream.

"So. Where have you been?!" she said, with her bright smile could that light up a dark room.

"I think the last time I saw you was at the Swiss in Tacoma, after you left Medi's," I said.

Josefina had been a bartender at the Swiss and I had just released The Secret Beast. I had given her a copy.

"I remember you were on your way to Texas!" she said.

"How is your yoga career going, you were just beginning, right?" I asked.

"It's going great. I'm teaching classes now," she said smiling. "I'm still working on my certification, I took a year off and was a flight attendant for Alaska Airlines."

"What?! How was that?" I said.

"Ah, it was all right. I was hoping to get to travel to cool places but it didn't work out that way. I want to travel on my own and do yoga instead. I went to Colombia last year," she said. "How's your writing going?"

"Really good, I released my second book called Doppelganger and am almost finished with a book I'm writing now called Bodhi," I said.

"Bodhi? That sounds interesting," she said.

"Do you live in Seattle now? I remember you were wanting to move here," I asked.

"Yep, I moved to West Seattle, but I'm looking to move closer to downtown where all my favorite yoga studios are at," she said.

"I need a photo for my new book cover, it has to be a Latina, and I nominate you. Are you into it?" I asked.

"Sure," she said.

I explained what I was looking for in the photo and told her to take a selfie and send it to me.

"No, you take it. I'm off on Wednesday, stop by my apartment around noon," she said.

"Excellent, text me your address," I said.

"So by the way, where are you living? What are you doing?" she asked.

"I just moved to Madison Valley, on the east side of Capitol Hill. My niece, Annie, had a beautiful two-bedroom unit on the main floor of a townhouse. It's close to downtown and is in a real quiet neighborhood," I said. "She works for Amazon and they sent her to Luxembourg for two years. I took over the unit and signed a new lease."

"Are you still painting and roofing?" she asked.

"I drive for Uber," I said.

Her face lit up.

"I bet you meet some interesting people and have

some crazy stories!" she said.

"It's kind of like picking up hitchhikers," I said.

"But you get paid for it! I've heard you can make great money doing that in this town," she said.

"Yeah. And I have this nice two-bedroom all to myself," I said.

"Do you want a roommate?" she asked.

I didn't speak for a moment.

As she turned to get another frosty glass, she looked back at me over her left shoulder and said "I'm serious, do you want a roommate?

I looked down at my empty pint-glass and then looked back up into her ravishing brown eyes.

"More Bodhi please," I said.

All is perception, everything a dream - Bodhi

ACKNOWLEDGMENTS

Edited by Norma "Rosie" Wigutoff

Cover Design by Brenna Pierce

Cover photo by Barbara Lopez

Made in the USA
Middletown, DE
22 December 2020

28368130R00136